The 30 DAY self perception *Makeover*®
TEEN EDITION

www.cathleneminer.com

Copyright © 2019

All rights reserved.

ISBN - 9781073728572

Published by Sawyere and the Sea, Inc.

Photo Credit by Kaitlin Rady unless otherwise noted

To all of the Teens out there that have that feeling deep
inside that they are going to do amazing things
with their lives...
You will...

Help and Support

In your journey or throughout this book, you may realize that you or someone you know needs help. We have included resources you can utilize to help yourself or those you love in this book. So many of us struggle through different issues as we grow into women. There are people and resources out there to help and support you where ever you live.

Some may be living in a home or are in dating situations that are emotionally and/or physically abusive. Domestic or dating violence is NOT OK. I have as set up a non profit to give Hope those who are getting back on their feet due to Domestic Violence and other detrimental situatons.
  Visit, www.hopefullhandbags.org for more information or to get involved.

Living in a violent home life, thoughts of suicide, drug use and drinking makes it very difficult to plan for the future.
Don't be afraid to let your friends, family, or teachers know what you need when they ask; they want to help. If you are currently residing in this kind of situation, it is important to communicate that to someone you trust or to reach out to one of the resources listed in this book. Under no circumstance should anyone be in physical or emotional danger.

One of the topics addressed in this book is self image. This particular topic has come up more often than any other throughout the research we have done for this book. It's completely normal to have a poor self image (we will guide you to change that in this book). However, many teens develop eating disorders due to an Unhealthy Self Image and Unhealthy Self Perception. It is our collective mission to give you resources to help.
A positive self image happens when we master a positive self perception. It is important to know that you are perfect just the way you are.

If you have any questions please email: info@hopefullhandbags.org and we will guide you towards the proper resolution. We genuinely care about you and your loved ones.
  Cathlene

Dedications & Gratitude

Cathlene

I would like to thank all of the experiences that I have been through as a Teen and in this life so far that led me to where I am today. I am now able to look back and realize how crucial a healthy Self Perception is and how to guide others to their own unique healthy Self Perception.

I am so grateful for my four children that taught me so much and gave me the opportunity to be their mom in this life. My now grown children, Tiler and Tayler, it's so exciting to me to see the amazing adults you have become and a joy to see that you have a Healthy Self Perception, I am happy it sunk in... I am grateful to my younger children, Emmett and Carolyne as they now go through their teenage years and have been going through The 30 Day Self Perception Makeover Teen Edition themselves. First-hand feedback... They have been guided with the tips and tricks you will find in this book to their Healthy Self Perception and trusting their intuition 100%.

My children helped me grow so much as a person and were such an inspiration for me to write this book. Thank you to my parents that have been my biggest cheerleader since day one.

My husband that always by my side with encouragement, positive vibes and stands beside me every single day cheering me on.

Kaitlin that took amazing pictures, edited and spent many many many hours by my side getting this book just right, Thank you!!!

And Thank you to Taelor, my co-author that let me in on her real-life everyday teen life and what it's like for most teens these days. And to the amazing teens, Marissa, Kate, Julia, Kaylee, Madie, Emercyn and Megha that took part in this book and gave me the real scoop on being a teen and the pressures that they are facing in today's world. Taelor and the amazing girls gave a lot of real life advice that I know you will all find helpful in your journey through this book and life.

I feel strongly that what holds people back from reaching their version of success and experiencing joy in their lives has everything to do with their Self Perception. I started Hopefull Handbags, Inc. Global to spread HOPE to women that are survivors of Domestic Violence and other detrimental Situations. We are raising awareness that Domestic Violence is NOT OK and that there is help and support all over the world. (More on Page 141) We are spreading the word that a Healthy Self Perception will allow you to realize and be aware if you are in a situation that you know is not right and not healthy. Recognizing a toxic situation is step one. There are many organizations that you can reach out to that will support and guide you to safety.

Your Self Perception dictates the path that your entire life takes and what you feel your worth is... Which by the way, you are worthy everything that you could ever dream of.

Taelor

Before I begin I want to first thank my head author, Mrs. Cathlene Miner and our editor and fabulous photographer Kaitlin Rady. Both of these amazing, beautiful, intelligent, and hardworking women have taught me so much about what it means to be the definition of an empowered young woman. I hold them so close and dear to my heart for the extraordinary opportunities I as a young adult have been exposed to. They have helped to guide me in this journey of co-authoring a book and teaching me all of the ins and outs of creating a life I desire for myself and to never settle for anything less than amazing. So, a million and more thank yous and love goes out to you two because, without you, no teen girl would be allowed the privilege in hearing what we have to say.

However, with that said; my mom, who could also be described as my number one supporter, my shoulder to lean on, and my best friend is who I give all credit to at the end of this journey. I have never met someone who is so caring and passionate about the things she loves. I don't know what I did to deserve such an amazing mother like you.

Growing up in this world and coming to understand the certain darkness it can hold makes me even more grateful to have had you by my side, regardless of its terrors. Thank you for leading me on this path to a beautiful life that I cannot wait to explore with you.

You bring so much light into my life as well as everyone around you, and no Taco Tuesday could be the same without you. Thank you for the endless laughs that make my stomach ache for hours and always being there for me when I need a moment to break down every once in a while. I'm so blessed that God gave me you. I believe that he knew we would be best friends forever. I love you so much.

How to use this book and information to benefit you the most.

This book is set up in days.
Days 1 -30.
If you feel that everyday is going to be a tough time commitment. Spread it out to maybe every other day.
Pick up where you left off.
Consistency is what will make the amazing shifts in your life.

It is all about your feelings, so if it doesn't feel good it will be counter productive. Now, that doesn't mean that some things may be not be uncomfortable... Change is uncomfortable. But when you have a healthy Self Perception and you see that because of your healthy Self Perception you are Manifesting your life on Purpose you will be Motivated and Inspired to keep going.

You've Got This!
And your Soulfully Fulfilled life is waiting for you to live it.

Please Join
Cathlene's
Online Community

For ongoing support throughout the processes of this book, and as a way to hold yourself accountabile, we highly recommend that you join our online communities. By signing up for our Manifesting Magic in Your Everyday Life blog or by linking up with one (or all) of our social media pages and groups, you will have access to amazing resources that further your development and also will be able to converse with girls and women who are going through the same processes you are.

Cathlene holds many live sessions and hosts a radio show that is dedicated to the manifesting, spiritual, and personal development of her followers. Be sure to post your self perception progress selfies with:

www.cathleneminer.com

i am living proof

about Cathlene

I'll let you in on a little something I don't talk about very much. I used to not think or feel very highly of myself at all. I thought I wasn't smart enough, thin enough, pretty enough, etc… I thought that everybody else had it all together and I wondered….what's wrong with me?

I avoided certain situations because I thought I just wasn't enough. I would see all of the popular girls at school and they "seemed" to be always smiling, so they must have it all together. Right?!

I had a terrible self-perception, but I hid it very well. As a teenager, I fell into a life of eating disorders. I would teeter back and forth between Anorexia and Bulimia. I thought I hid it well. Young women (and even adult women) are good at faking it when we need to, aren't we?

My mom caught on, as moms do. She brought me to counseling and all of the things a great mother would do but as much as I heard what they were telling me from a clinical perspective, it was really what I thought and felt about myself that kept me trapped in that place in my mind. I later figured out it was a disconnect from my intuitive self and my subconscious mind that believed all of the things that society was feeding me.

As far as I knew no one at school knew I had an eating disorder except my boyfriend at the time. He really did try and help but I was living a life in my head based on untruths.
I thought-
The girls at school that were thinnest were happy.
The girls at school that had the boys chasing them were happy. I felt that some of the girls at school looked down on me because I was me.

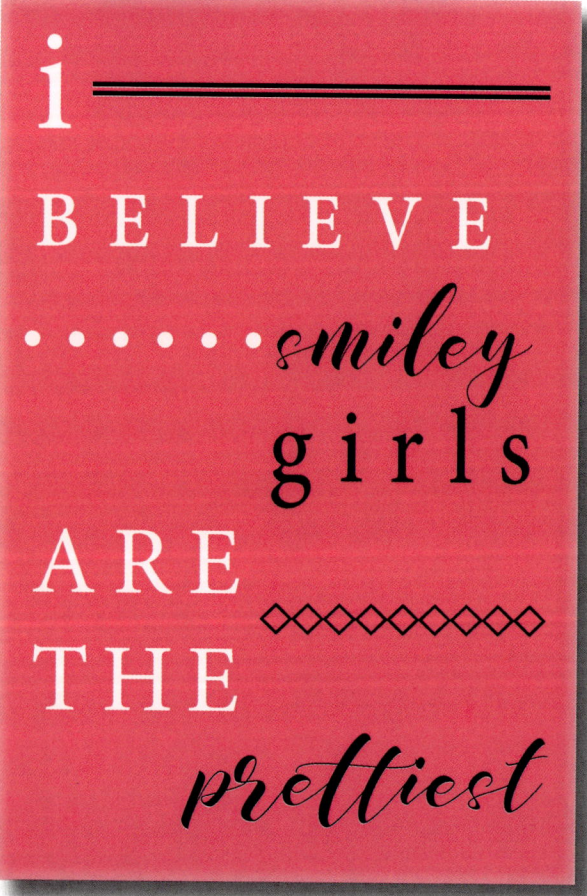

i BELIEVE smiley girls ARE THE prettiest

The funny thing is I always knew deep down (my Intuitive Self) that these things were not true, but I would talk myself out of believing it. That intuition that I was so connected with and trusted as a young child was like a voice that I wish would go away sometimes.

It felt like a constant battle in my head.

Even in my high school days, I was very independent. I started working when I was 15 because I wanted to pay for my own things. As a teenager, I would help others with my earnings and volunteer my time. I've always gotten great satisfaction from helping others.

So, even though I didn't have a healthy Self-perception and was suffering from an eating disorder, I was still very involved and present. Not many knew what I was struggling with on the inside. I was battling with myself every single day in my head, but on the outside, I seemed fine.

I would base my day on how I felt about me and how I felt about me was not good at all. I would look in the mirror every day and criticize something. Instead of telling myself how amazing I was, I would tell myself the exact opposite.

> *"I would base my day on how I felt about me and how I felt about me was not good at all."*

I thought I wanted to be like everyone else, or should I say my ego self wanted to be like everyone else. My Intuitive self knew that I was a born leader. Deep down I knew that I was great just the way that I was. I always had a feeling that I was born to do a lot in this world. I was born to help others.

As a teenager, I was not in alignment with who I was put here to be, nor what I was here to do and it was very uncomfortable. We are here to bring out the best in ourselves first. When we accomplish this, we begin to bring out the best in the people around us. We are in this life to be our authentic selves and compliment each other, figuratively and literally.

● ● ● ● ● ● ● ●

As an adult, I became much healthier physically, I worked in a Medical Facility and had two part time jobs. I became a fitness coach and personal trainer; and cleaned houses on the weekends to provide for my children, but I did not let this bog me down. However I some challenges (At least I thought they were at the time). See, I had two children at a very young age and I went through a divorce at a young age as well. I was always working and I knew that something had to change. I was meant for more. I began realizing that when it came to the things that I most loved and enjoyed those circumstances were falling into place beautifully. This is when I truly started building the life that I desired. I began manifesting on purpose. I started to pay attention to every feeling that I had. Every thought that came to my mind.

I started feeling myself climbing out of my funk. Journaling and meditating for a few minutes every morning was once again showing its rewards. I was getting back into my alignment.

Soon, I was attracting everything I desired. I marrried an amamzing man and that beautiful home I had been envisioning and journaling about was my reality.

I felt at a high vibe frequency most of the time and when I wasn't, I knew how to get myself out of the funk quickly.

Manifesting on Purpose, I would go to my journal and Check, Check, Check, did that, got that, I see that...(more on that later too).

I became a stay at home mom (which was a whole new world for me) and my husband and I were excited to have two more children. While I was certainly living the life I created, I began to get bogged down once again. I had manifested all of the help I needed, but again life needed to change. I was evolving.

That's when the light bulb went off and I realized NOW was the TIME! Why do I keep allowing myself to get into the funks when I know that I am creating and manifesting all of this. What I focus on grows.

"I began realizing that when it came to the things that I most loved and enjoyed those circumstances were falling into place. And more and more opportunities relating to those and my passions were presented in front of me. This is when I truly started building the life that I desired. I began manifesting on purpose."

As a teenager, if you can master this mindset you will reach whatever height you set your mind to. We were not meant to stay in one place like rocks, but to flow like rivers. We grow within ourselves and spread our wings to achieve things that fulfill our souls even more. Limitlessness.

The purpose of you doing all of the work in this book is to make it so that you don't have to wait any longer to know that this life is limitless. Now is your time.

So, here we are in your now. Now is the time to figure out what fills your heart and soul, that's what you are here in this life to do. It's time to figure out what lights you up. It's time to plant in your subconscious mind that down times and plateaus are a time for re-evaluation, not failure, not the end.

Keep in mind, that as you grow and change as a woman, what lights you up will change and evolve. Your growth and change will keep evolving throughout your life. That's completely natural and even expected. We are going to get you tapped into what you are feeling, get you acquainted and familiar with your intuition, and transform your self-perception into one that is full of love, knows its worth, and has admiration for you.

What is the trick to living the life you desire? The answer is to live in the "now". Now is the time to hone in on your passions and take inspired action to follow them. Now is the time to wake up each morning excited for the day ahead. Now is the time to be excited for the life ahead.

I paid attention to the things that shifted in my life. I realized that some things in my life worked exactly as I desired. And those "things" were what excited me and made me smile.

I was high vibe about all of my ideas and got excited. So, guess what? They became my new reality!

I reconnected with my inner guidance and listened, watched for signs - listened to messages the universe put in front of me. I felt like I was finally on the path to my purpose, the reason I am here, now.

My children even began to look at the world differently. They adopted a glass half full mentality because they were also learning the power of a great self-perception.

After some inspired work (that I am giving you the secrets to in this book!), my life did a complete 180-degree turn. I realized that I created my life. I do have control over it. I trusted my intuition and suddenly had the "perfect for me" relationships enter my life.

I took inspired action and money flowed in. The place I desired to live became my home. By the way, that is only the tip of the iceberg. Even the people closest to me saw shifts in their lives. My high energy vibe influenced their lives too!

Now, I want to help you make that same 180-degree turn. Allow your life to work in your favor. If you are consistent, you will see results.

I'm now living where I have always desired to live. I have an amazing husband, four beautiful children, and two beautiful grandchildren. My passions came together into a successful business that I love. I give back through the charity I founded, Hopefull Handbags, Inc., Global.(More on Page 143)

I figured out how to create the life of my dreams. I took everything I learned during this period and put it into this signature TEEN Self-Perception Makeover. I am so excited to give this to you so you can practice it in your life. Start creating and living the life of your dreams. Once you work on your self-perception, your life will shift in your favor.

It is important to be reminded that down times in life happen for everyone, even me sometimes here and there. When it does happen to me, I am reminded to show gratitude for all I have achieved in life. Looking at the good and being thankful will attract the good back to you.

Tough seasons are great for learning what we are all truly capable of, helping us learn how to identify the good. It is okay to feel down but do not set up camp there. Know that things will turn around for you and keep focusing on all the "high vibes" will get you where you desire to go. This journey we are about to take will get you there.

> Tough seasons are great for learning what we are all truly capable of, helping us learn how to identify the good. It is okay to feel down but do not set up camp there. Know that things will turn around for you and keep focusing on all the "high vibes" will get you where you desire to go. This journey we are about to take will get you there.

let's get personal

about Taelor

Hello to the beautiful soul reading this right now. Allow me to introduce myself:
My name is Taelor Mabry and I am just a 17 year old girl, maybe like yourself. I am writing this today in hopes to create a connection or a friendship, if you will, as you read through this book, because no matter the situation, no one should be in it alone.

So this is me.

I am originally a California girl but as the times changed, I now find myself in beautiful Florida. Where I have grown up, made friends, and truly found myself. I have created a picture of what the rest of my near future holds. However, the universe may have different plans for me, but this is what I've got so far…

My plan, (ooohhh the life consuming plannn) as us highschoolers may approach it, is to graduate high school, have the most amazing summer with those I love, and go off to college and start the next chapter of my life fresh and ready to create the long lasting college memories we all may dream of. I hope to study American Sign Language, Deaf Education, and Interpreting. Farther down the road I hope to travel to other countries and give language to those who may not have it, and just to spread this beautiful art form. I have always had a passion for helping people and when the exquisite art of Sign Language fell into my lap my freshman year, I knew it was something I was passionate about.

If I could give any piece of advice to anyone who is struggling with their "big college decision" I would have to say go down the path you are most passionate about, because when it is right in your heart and in your bones you can feel it, the universe, your God, or whatever you lay your hopes, wishes, and dreams in will reciprocate that for you. Doors will open for you, and who knows, you may find a new passion you never even knew you had.

Aside from all this crazy college talk, while I am still in high school my other passions and hobbies are volleyball, writing, English, killing the grade game, and making memories and having fun during football season! To anyone reading this: GET INVOLVED!!! You will thank me later for it. Some things I have been involved in so far is the Yearbook club, the Literature magazine, Ascension club, and just all the sports fun! Each of these things have helped me thrive in high school. The everlasting friendships I have made, the connections between faculty and staff (shoutout to my amazing English teacher Mr. Rick Ryan), and all the school spirit and pride has changed my high school experience for me completely and I hope in reading this, you will too!! When they say it is the best years of your life, it's true. At least so far.

Here, I can't lie. As high school is the best four years of our lives, there are always obstacles. May it be in schoolwork, or in our own heads, it will always be there. Going through this book, I want you to find things that appeal to you and make you feel good. Use them as tools to get through these obstacles and grow and thrive to become the most beautiful and strong you. Because, when I started high school and walked in on that very first day, I was not half as confident as I am now; in my body and everything else that made me. I have grown so much with the help of my family and my best friends and I have so much to thank for that. You are all so amazing and special to me. Without you, none of this would have been possible.

So… this is me. I hope we know each other a little bit better now and you yourself and grow with me too. It really is a fun ride. Go kill it babe!!

XO,
Tae

TABLE OF CONTENTS

About Authors	Page 5
Introduction	Page 14
3 Vibrational Frequencies Explained	Page 16
Definitions to Know	Page 17
Cathlene's Bubble Theory	Page 17
First Things First	Page 18
Day One - Take Inspired Action	Page 26
Day Two - Finding a New Perspective	Page 30
Day Three - Giving, Receiving, and Personality	Page 34
Day Four - Becoming a Manifesting Master	Page 38
Day Five - Doing Everyday Right	Page 42
Day Six - The Joy in the Journey	Page 46
Day Seven - Action vs. Inspired Action	Page 50
Day Eight - The Definition of Beauty	Page 54
Day Nine - You are Limitless	Page 56
Day Ten - Giving Compliments	Page 60
Day Eleven - Receiving Compliments	Page 62
Day Twelve - Addressing Self Sabotage	Page 64
Day Thirteen - The Gift in a Smile	Page 68
Day Fourteen - The Letter	Page 72
Day Fifteen - The Habits that Move You Forward	Page 74
Day Sixteen - Feeling Your Best	Page 78
Day Seventeen - Ego Self vs. Intuitive Self	Page 82
Day Eighteen - Your Body Image	Page 86
Day Nineteen - Your Posture	Page 90
Day Twenty - What You Love About You	Page 94
Day Twenty-one - What If?	Page 96
Day Twenty-two - You are Amazing	Page 100
Day Twenty-three - Your Worth	Page 102
Day Twenty-four - How You Perceive Others	Page 106
Day Twenty-five - Compliment Yourself	Page 110
Day Twenty-six - Dreaming and Manifesting	Page 114
Day Twenty-seven - What Others Think	Page 118
Day Twenty-eight - Your Empty Space	Page 120
Day Twenty-nine - Life and Lessons	Page 124
Day Thirty - Forgiving Yourself	Page 126
Bonus Day - Your Self Confidence	Page 128
Where to go from here	Page 132
Who is Cathlene	Page 135
Affirmations	Page 136
Resources	Page 138

Hey Girl...this is for us.

We live in a world full of filters and scroll through pictures of lives that appear to be real, but are airbrushed. It seems like everything around us shouts perfection and somehow that makes us feel...well, incredibly imperfect. There is no Facebook, Instagram, or Snapchat filter available to really show the beauty that's below the make-up, the contouring, or the carefully chosen outfits. Of course, we know that we run deeper than all of that.

But how do we keep up?

The fact is, we have been trading our own destinies and how we feel about ourselves for the dreams and opinions of others. It's time for us to reclaim that gorgeous goddess within and begin manifesting our lives...on purpose. After all, now is the time! Now is always the time.

As young women, we have so much resting on our shoulders. There is so little time for rest, sleep, and reflection when we have a schedule that's filled to the brim with other obligations. It feels like the only time we have for ourselves is spent in front of the mirror in the morning and in the evening.

That time is almost counterproductive because we spend it picking ourselves apart.

What if I lost ten pounds?

What if I was funnier?

What if I was faster?

What if my grades were better?

What if I wasn't so socially awkward?

What if (this is a big one) I was just like "someone else"?

If only our mirrors made us look like how we portray ourselves on social media. Wouldn't that be phenomenal? I'm asking us to go deeper. Deeper into who we are and really push ourselves onto the path that we know is for us. The path that leads to fulfillment and abundance in every way.

We already shine like there is #nofilter needed. The real beauty IS in the mirror and in the soul within our beautiful bodies.

There is a secret I want to share with you through this book. We have the ability to create the life and obtain the things we really desire. We must first understand, realize, and feel that which we are worthy and what we desire. There will be words I want you to keep as far away from you as possible as we go through this process.

Words Like:
Never
Can't
Won't
Hate
Ugly
Want
Might

From now on, we don't use those words in the context that describes ourselves or our situation. Words are powerful. They are a reflection of our mindset and an indicator of our future.

I would like you to also set your intentions for this book and how you want it to impact your life. This process will require you to intentionally set time aside for yourself. This is something that is sometimes hard to do with our school, sports, friends and family, and work schedules. However, this is a great practice for us to get into now so that we can carry the habit of valuing our alone time and ourselves into adulthood.

Put a reminder in your phone or your planner. Set aside at least 30 minutes any time during the day that works best for you. You will need to do this in a place that makes you feel peaceful and gives you the liberty to really dive into yourself. I want you to feel completely safe, loved, and open when you are going through the pages of this book or while you are completing your journal entries and other activities outlined. Choose a time that will work for most days for consistency and routine.

Since we can choose our words…then we can also choose our futures. That is exactly what we are going to do.

GIRL,
you've got GOOD vibes!

Did you know that everything around us is comprised of energy and frequency? What we put out into the world, we get back on the same energy frequency level. In this book, I am going to teach you how to use that energy and harness frequency to get what you desire and live an explosively divine led life. A life where you listen to your intuition. A life where you recognize your intuition and listen to it 100% of the time. I want you to live your purposefully knowing that you have everything you need for success already hard wired in that beautiful body, brain and soul of yours.

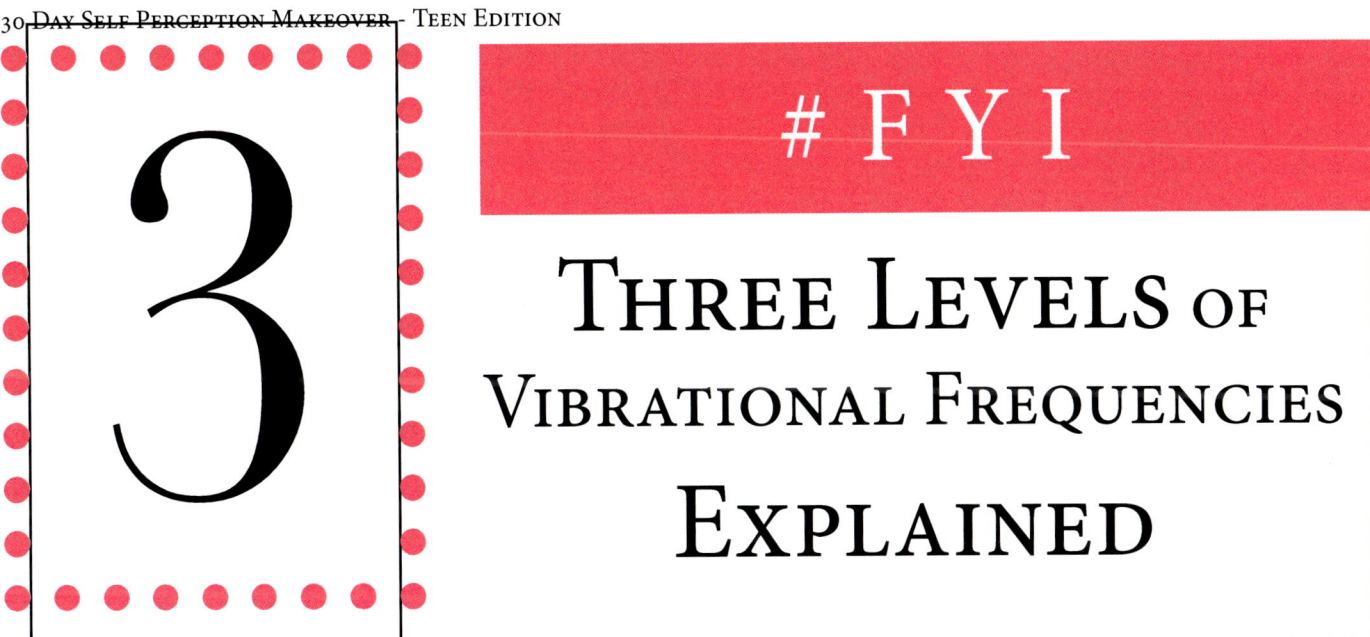

#FYI
Three Levels of Vibrational Frequencies Explained

High Vibes: Things are better than smooth sailing. You feel that life and circumstances are aligning. Doors are opening. Opportunity is chasing you down.
You may even find yourself saying to yourself, "This is too good to be true."
Recognize this even when the thought comes up. This will begin to lower your energy frequency. Change it to: This is good and this is true. Leave it at that. Do not think too much into this. When we interact with God (Universe), we always want to think "this or better".

Middle (Mediocre): This is when things are just okay. Your schoolwork is getting done and you feel okay about your friendships. You are "somewhat" healthy. Overall, you just feel very middle of the road and feel as if you can get better.

This is where most of society stays. This is stuck or on a plateau. Know that you can go up from here and this is why you are doing this book. Even a twinge in the "up" direction will begin to open your flow more than it is right now.

Low (Lessons): Here, you are mainly feeling down, anxious, depressed. You feel as if nothing is going your way. Now, it is time to recognize that you are on a low energy frequency vibration and the thoughts you have must change.

The changed thoughts will lead to changed feelings, which will in turn get your energy frequency vibrations going in the "up" direction. This is when being in the middle of a low and mediocre energy frequency is ok. You are headed in the right direction.

Just like stated in the Mediocre energy frequency vibration; Even a twinge in the "up" vibrational direction is a great start!

Your feelings are a good indicator of where your vibration is set. Now, I'm not saying you're not going to have bad days or even bad feelings. That's not really what I'm talking about here (though it still very much matters!) In this case, we are talking about our general feeling about outcomes.

Focusing on positive outcomes, positive interactions, and positive opportunities and being excited about the future will yield that higher vibe you are looking for and attract solutions, great people, and great circumstances. Ever notice that the people that have a "nothing good ever happens…or…nothing works out" attitude generally do live a life where nothing good happens or nothing works out for them? Where your focus lies is generally what we can expect (what you focus on grows).

Definitions to Know

<u>Universe/God</u>: As referred to in this book. Most people believe that God created the Universe. Therefore they are as one. Whichever word resonates with you and your belief is what you should use.

<u>Meditation/Prayer</u>: Sitting quietly or speaking to your inner guidance or higher power.

<u>Manifesting</u>: Creating, Magnetizing... be evidence of; prove

<u>Self Perception</u>: What you think and feel about yourself. Not what anyone else thinks or feels about you.

<u>Self Love</u>: What you do to nurture your own well being.

<u>Self Worth</u>: Your own value. What you think you deserve

<u>Limiting beliefs and blocks</u>: Those thoughts and feelings which constrain us or hold us back in some way. They are thoughts and feelings that our subconscious mind believes to be true although there is no truth to them. They were given to us by others in our past or past circumstances and we believe them as truth.

Cathlene's "Bubble" Theory

A Must for Every Day,
Place a clear bubble around you every morning visually. This bubble lets positivity in and the negative feeling and vibrations to bounce right off and dissolve into the Universe.

You will visually imagine those negative, not so great feelings and thoughts bounce off of your bubble and dissolve into the Universe.

After your quiet sitting time actually imagine a clear bubble surrounding you. Put Sparkles in it, flowers, whatever feels right to you. Imagine it soft and bouncy. When you encounter a negative person or comment through out the day do not let it in. Visualize it bouncing off of your bubble and dissolving into the Universe. You do not need it... it is not serving you... You have let it go.

> "Try new things, step out of your comfort zone, take risks, do things in ways you've never done them before, ask for help, surround yourself with self-actualized people, become obsessed with the fact that you have one go-round on this planet as the you that is you, and realize how precious and important it is not to squander that."
> -Jen Sincero

first things first
THE VISION BOARD

We are going to have so much fun with this project! A vision board is a visual representation of what we want in our lives. This can include anything you want tomorrow and vary to what you might want ten years down the road. I know that I get clippings from images I search for on the internet, magazines, or books.

Think of the life that you desire and dream of as something that will happen...not something that might happen. A vision board is not done with "wishful" thinking, but with "knowing" thinking. Every time you place a picture on your vision board, feel as if it has already happened. A vision board is a time where you dream big. Nothing is holding you back here. Time, money circumstances, geography, people. Nothing...

FOR EXAMPLE:

Claire really desires to get into the University of Massachusetts. She's been dreaming about this for so long. As she puts together her vision board, she places the picture of the Student Hall on her vision board, and closes her eyes so she can see herself there.

She feels her feet on the sidewalk walking into the building. Claire feels the excitement rising within her as she opens the front doors and smells that familiar old book scent. She walks through hallways enamored with symbols and crests of her dream college. She is excited to know the people she will meet and the see the places she will go. Claire knows that she is worthy and deserves this university. She also knows why she wants this particular education.

That's how we really amplify and expedite motivation and goals. We are already there before we are there. Even if we aren't sure exactly why we want something (that's pretty typical and understandable), we know that it's something that we must do. This is our Intuitive Self giving us messages too!

We don't have to have everything figured out all at once. Life is not like a blueprint that an architect designs and places in front of us, directing us where to go and how to build. We are the authors and creators of our own destinies. We all have the divine capability to direct our paths and form the life we were made to design.

The aspirations and goals that you have are unique to you and point you in the direction of your ultimate purpose. The feelings that will soulfully fill you in this life. They are not there so that you can fail at them or not achieve them. They are there because they are 100% possible and you are deserving of the outcomes that put you further on your path to them.

You can purchase material for your vision board at any arts and crafts store. The board should be large and placed in a spot where you can see it everyday. The point of this exercise is to immerse ourselves in our dreams (not the dreams or hopes of others around us) and to train our minds to stay positive.

Keep in mind, that your board will likely change as you tap deeper into yourself and become more aware of your own desires. That's okay! I would hope that would be the case.

Here are some ideas for what to think about when putting together your vision board:

- *What do I desire my friendships to feel and look like?*
- *What college or career do I desire to have?*
- *What kind of healthy food do I think is best for the health of my body?*
- *What kind of exercise or sport do I really want to excel at?*
- *What do I desire the relationship with my family members to feel like?*
- *What dress or outfit do I really desire right now?*
- *Where do I desire to travel?*
- *What country is the most interesting to me?*
- *What habit do I wish to have or be more consistent with?*
- *If I could live in any house or apartment, what would it look, what will it feel like?*
- *What does a strong, independent, and happy woman look and feel like to me?*
- *Keep in mind that it is all about how you desire a situation or thing to make you feel. It's not about having the actual situation or thing.*

"The secret of having it all is believing you already do."
-Anonymous

journaling 101

Journaling will be a huge routine while you go through each day outlined in this book. When we create our lives, writing everything down serves multiple purposes and also requires using different parts of your brain, therefore, retraining your subconscious mind at a faster, more efficient pace. Start this book with a brand new journal. Decorate the cover like you decorate the vision board. Make it colorful and fun and a true expression of the fabulous you.

#1) Aligning ourselves for success...

When we write down our feelings and emotions or our dreams and aspirations, we are aligning ourselves in a multidimensional way to attain that which we desire. Visually, mentally, and physically.

Writing down fears, anxieties, or issues you might have gives you the opportunity to see them and then let them go. It will also allow you to switch certain thought patterns around that are not serving you. Writing down where we desire to be and what we desire to experience in our lives allows us to see them on paper and visualize them.

#2) Telling the Universe that you're ready...

When we put forth an action with a clear intention, the Universe immediately gets to work to assist us. Whether it's getting something we desire or changing a negative mindset. By getting a journal (or even putting together a vision board) and writing in it, we are setting energy in motion towards what we really desire.

When you write down what you desire throughout this process, make sure that you are truly tapping into the feelings that go along with it. For example, if what you desire is to get into a particular college, write down what it's going to feel like to be accepted. How did the acceptance letter look and how did it feel to read through it?

Visualize yourself in your mind being excited and opening the letter! It's exciting, right? So, be excited!

#3) Letting go...

Through journaling we are able to let go of emotions and/or even begin the process of forgiveness or start a process of healing. Your intentions should always be to let go and receive better. When we are aware of our emotions and feelings and begin to harness them as tools to win instead of things that bring us down, we empower ourselves and give ourselves permission to not be afraid of what we perceive as "negative."

Think of emotions as nerve endings in our bodies. If it did not hurt to touch a stovetop, we wouldn't know that it is harmful for our hands. Sometimes, we must feel negative emotions so we can pinpoint an area that needs to be worked on or healed within ourselves. Sometimes, negative emotions are alerting us that a situation is not good for us or even that a relationship no longer has a purpose in our lives.

Letting go of these emotions through journaling allows us to process through their meaning and also to not be afraid of sadness, grief, or even anger. It's okay to feel negative feelings, but we don't set our camp there. We converse with them, ask God or our angels for guidance, and allow ourselves to be guided towards resolution.

#4) Visualizing

Visualizing is so key in this process. Our subconscious mind does not know the difference between what is real and what is not. By visualizing your desires and visualizing you already in that place, feeling those feelings, you are opening your flow wide open to receive those things.

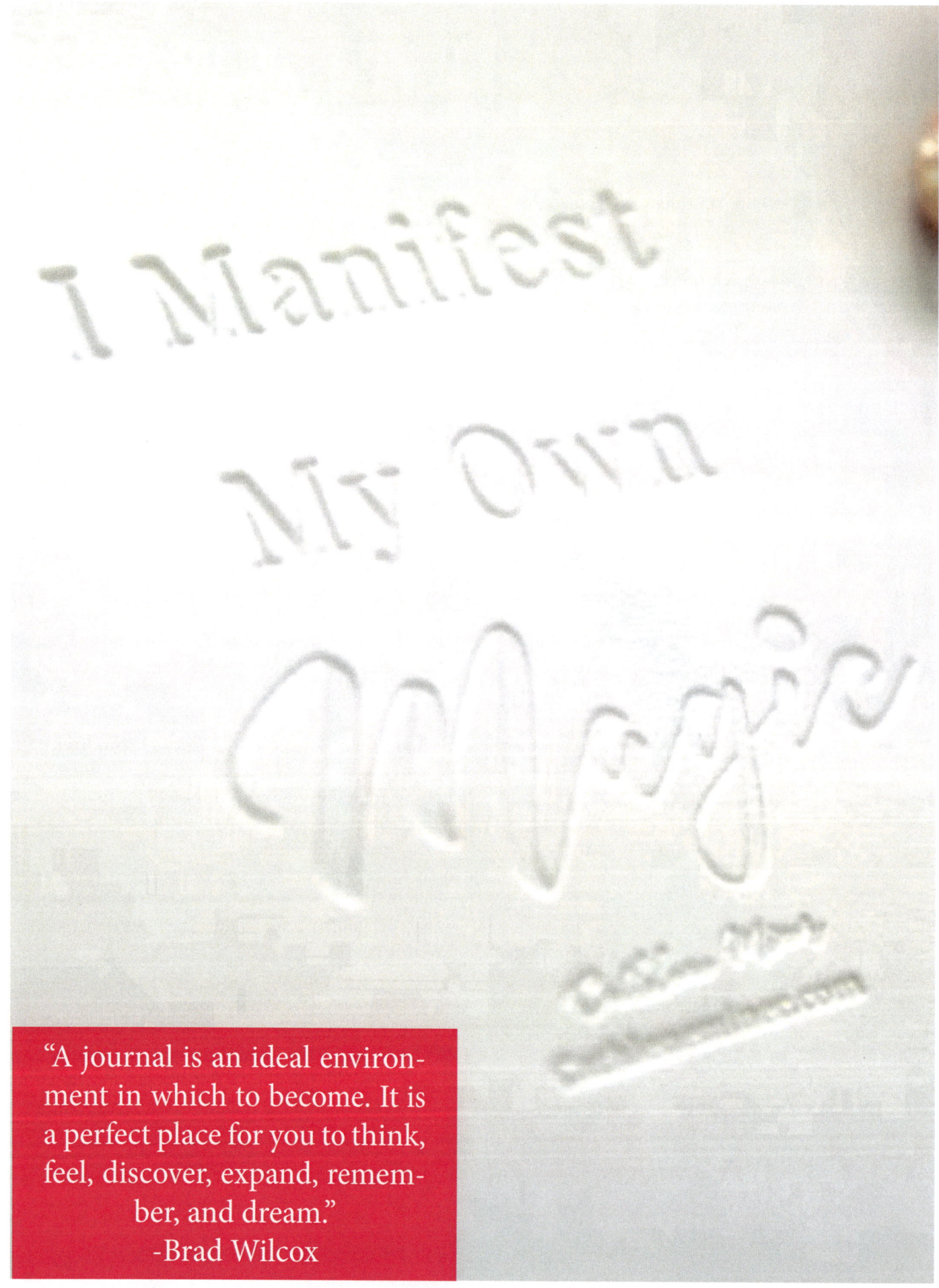

> "A journal is an ideal environment in which to become. It is a perfect place for you to think, feel, discover, expand, remember, and dream."
> -Brad Wilcox

you are worthy...affirm your life

You are worthy...

You are worthy of the best life you could ever imagine. You are worthy of happiness, success, and people that love and respect you in your life. Through this process, you'll realize that you are worthy of more than what you can even imagine! Yes, you!

Each one of us has the ability and capability to receive the blessings and abundance stored up and planned for us, but in order to open the door to that abundance we must have our feelings and vibrations aligned to them. Feeling unworthy or undeserving blocks that flow.

Working on our self perception is integral to this process.

How we feel and think about ourselves shapes our realities. This is why the first step to really creating (manifesting) your life on purpose first starts within.

Think of abundance as a Christmas present that is wrapped up and put under the tree. If you never open it, you will never receive it. You won't enjoy that one gift that you've been really thinking of. Think of a positive self image as opening up that gift. Tearing the wrapping apart with excitement.

Think to yourself and say out loud:
I am worthy of wonderful things!
I am worthy of abundance!
I am worthy of health!
I am worthy of beautiful friendships!
I am worthy of my goals!
I am worthy of my dreams!

As you are saying these affirmations, visualize each one of the uniquely for you. Visualize and feel that wonderful thing and so on...

See page (136) for more affirmations

Affirm your life...

Accept where you are right now in your life. Accept the reality where you are and know that you have all of the power to change it.

Acknowledge all that has happened in the past, accept that those things have led you to where you are right now. Reading this book. Changing your life and opening your flow for your desires to freely come your way.

Own your story.

Own your past, your present, and get ready to own the life you are manifesting.

the "no fear" lifestyle

Be Without Fear

Fear is a main component in blocking us from the destiny we absolutely deserve and should have. Fear is comprised of many things. Sometimes fear happens because of bad things we have experienced in our past, things we have witnessed happen to others, or bad things that people have told us about.

Fear is a liar.

Fear tells us we are not good enough, not smart enough, not attractive enough, and/or not athletic enough, the list can go on. The truth is, we are enough. That is what this book is all about. It's about removing the filters and the fear and walking fully into life equipped with exactly what we need.

That is us...you.

When you feel that others are saying you can not do it or have it. Or they say you're dreaming too big.

> First off there is never anything too big. Dream big honey and than dream some more…

Sometimes it will be the people closest to you that we feel are not supportive or they are telling us that they do not think we can do that. Keep in mind that sometimes it's from their fear. Their fear for you. Sometimes the people that love us the most have such a protective feeling that they do not want us to get hurt or fail.

That's okay. They are allowed to have those feelings. But, that is their feeling, their emotion, you do not have to take it on. Send love energetically to that person knowing that they are coming from a place of love. Do not give any more thoughts to their emotion of fear.

You will also have some that are coming from a place of jealousy. Jealousy and comparison are negative energy vibration. Let that bounce off of your clear bubble for sure.

So, now...

To get the most out of this book and to shift your self-perception you need to put yourself first. This isn't selfish. You're more helpful to everyone else when you put yourself first. When you are connecting, aligning and working on you, you are are radiating out at a higher energy frequency. This is not ego driven at all. In fact it's the opposite, so never feel like you are being selfish for putting you first.

After all, it's the people in this world that take care of themselves first and that have a healthy Self Perception that are able to help others and change the world for the better.

You radiate out at a higher energy frequency level because your needs have been met. You have spent the time on nurturing you. Imagine that every time you to take an action for someone else or inspired action towards a goal, that you are overflowing from a full cup, not pouring out. Everyone around you will notice a change. Sometimes they are not even sure what's different. They just know that something is and it's pretty amazing.

You will also notice that some of the people you are closest to are shifting their lives as well for the better. Your energies are radiating out so strong that it is having a compound effect. You may notice that some people are drifting away (more on this below). This can be hard sometimes, because we love our friends and the relationships we have in our lives.

sometimes, things change...

How relationships may change when you put out this "new positive energy," and how to handle it.

You may notice that some people begin to inch away when you start radiating out at a higher energy level. They know something has changed, they just cannot pinpoint what's different. They are not sure why they feel a bit uncomfortable.

This uncomfortable feeling from them is because you are radiating out at a higher energy frequency. They are no longer aligned with the same energy that you are.

Why?

Because you are now focused on more of the positive, a cup half full approach. You are more secure, confident, and purposefully driven than you were before.

People that are typically negative don't want to feel alone in their negativity. So, when you all of a sudden are not interested in feeding into their negativity and having a pity party with them, those people will start inching away. To be honest, it will likely be you choosing to inch away.

If you find that some of your friends are becoming more distant, do a little happy dance. This is something that I personally love, because it allows you to weed out negativity in your life without too much effort, just by following your intuition…!

This is happening so that your desires begin to align. Do not question it.

Don't resist and try to fix or bring those people closer.

However, you may, in fact, be the very person that lights the way for the others around you by inspiring them to look inward and make positive shifts in their lives even if it's after they have inched away.

This is the universe getting you where you are meant to be and making room.
Trust the process.

How much time will this makeover take?

This will only take 15 to 30 minutes out of your entire day! If you find yourself making more time for it, even better. It is so worth it, and when you start seeing amazing results you'll be motivated to keep on going. You will see changes in your life that you never imagined.

The changes that will begin to happen around you with circumstances and people will astound you and keep you motivated to keep going.

Consistency is key. As long as you make this a priority and it happens every day, with consistency, you will begin seeing shifts in your life for the better.

secret manifesting tip

A Cathlene Exclusive

In working with myself and my clients, I've found in order to retrain the subconscious mind it initially takes 18 seconds for a thought to stick. So, be sure that you are spending 18 seconds on thoughts and feelings that allow you to radiate out at a higher frequency. This opens you to the flow that manifests your desires into your life NOW and brings those circumstances and people into your life that are on the same high energy frequency. More tips on this as you go through the book...

"Celebrate each and every small shift for how amazing it really is."
- Cathlene

Day 1
Taking Inspired Action

"I guess I know that I want my life to change, but I don't really know where to start most of the time. Pretty much every morning, I start picking myself apart. It's like my day starts in the mirror. I feel like there's always someone else that's more talented, prettier, and smarter. It's hard for me to think of feeling different about myself."
Natasha, age 15

I hear yah, Natasha! Let's start by taking inspired action right away. After all, it's only when we take inspired action that things actually change.

Get the journal that you have hopefully decorated and made your very own. The first entry in your journal for this 30 Day Makeover is: What do you think about yourself and your physical appearance? Positive or negative, just let it flow out of you and onto the paper. Don't stop writing. Do not question what you are writing.

It might be hard for you to do this at first. After all, we are our harshest critics. Also, other young women (even our friends) are very hard on the people around them sometimes too. We all have experienced dirty looks, betrayal in friendships, and constant comparison. It can be hard to be real with ourselves when we feel like we can't be real with others without risking getting hurt. Remember this though, we want to look and feel good for ourselves only. This journey is for you!

The most important part of your writing process during this entry (and all entries) is to understand that during this time there is no judgment. Everything you write in this journal belongs to you and it is beautiful. Even the not so great truths that you express. The important thing to remember is that you are flowering. You are unfolding. You are exploding!

After you have written everything down, take a little break and take deep breaths. Once you feel centered, return to the entry and begin changing over your statements and looking at them from a glass half full mentality. Taking the time to change over your statements is a crucial part of the success of this program - and essential to nurturing a positive self perception.

This retrains your subconscious mind. Consistency and repetition, along with visualizing and feeling as if you are already in these places and situations, is very important.

The brain is complex, but very simple...Like every muscle. It does exactly what you tell it to do.

Change Over Statements
You can do this!

Here are a few examples of how changed over statements may look:

I am not skinny. Not nearly as skinny as some of my friends. I wish my arms didn't look the way they did in strapless dresses and my legs weren't so big.

I am in the exact place I am meant to be right now in this life. I am taking inspired action to feel good again. It does not matter what my friends looks like, because how they look does not define my beauty. My arms and legs are beautiful and work to do amazing things for me.

I am not worthy or deserving.

I so deserve this life that I live and all of the wonderful things that are heading my way. Blessing and favor chases me wherever I go. I was put in this life for a unique reason. I am here to experience all of the amazing opportunities (you manifest them!) that come my way.

I am not liked sometimes (others are jealous - misery likes company):

The right people are put in my life at the right times.

I let go of the toxic relationships not meant to be in my life any longer to make room for the amazing people that are on the way. I deserve healthy, uplifting, and balanced relationships. I no longer hang out or entertain those who make me feel negatively or that use me for their own purposes.

I am here for you if you need a little more guidance on change over statements. You have access to this video:

Go to https://www.cathleneminer.com/30day where I explain how to change over your statements.

We all have areas to work on about how we think about ourselves. This process gets us closer to pinpointing those concerns.

To fix anything, we first need to know what needs fixing!

"Growing up is hard! Having great friends along the way makes it easier! Be kind to everyone and make sure to be confident in who you are! Self-love is the best love!"
-Kate

Notes
for your eyes only

> Being optimistic with yourself and your life has such a huge impact on who you are as a person. In every broken situation, something beautiful blossoms out of it! I love how this book includes being so positive with yourself. Optimism and confidence with yourself lead to the boldness to spread light and positivity to others too!
> -Madie

30 Day Self Perception Makeover - Teen Edition

> I think it's really important to find things that help you re-charge and re-balance yourself. Like, sometimes I get really busy so I like to do things that help me to recharge like drawing & sketching. That way, I don't ever feel overwhelmed or stressed. Mom and I also try to make sure I balance things so that I'm not working on too many projects at the same time. I think when I'm able to focus on only one project, it comes out way better than if I was trying to juggle a bunch of projects, and then that makes me feel really good knowing that I completed a goal and I didn't have to stress out about it.
> -Celai

Day 2: Finding New Perspective

"When I go through my Instagram and Facebook feed, sometimes it's just a reminder of what I am not. I'm pretty confident for the most part, I guess, but there are days when I don't feel like I'm living up to the standards of pretty much everybody. It's just a lot of pressure and I'm tired of trying to live up to something that wasn't even my choice or idea in the first place."
Jenyfer, age 15

As teenagers, we adjust ourselves to fit into a mold set before us and most of the time we feel like we come up lacking. Social media, society, people in school, and sometimes even our families put a lot of pressure on us to be a reflection of what they want us to be instead of encouraging us to be who we really are. Snapchat filters and our Instagram news feeds are filled to the brim with pictures depicting a perfect life.

We find ourselves constantly comparing ourselves to others' bodies, to their perfect teeth, and their perfect outfits even when we know that those pictures and posts are just a snapshot of real life. And they are a very airbrushed version at that.

Selfies have ironically turned into a thing for others. How many likes we get on a post drastically changes how we feel about ourselves and can even alter how we feel through the day.

I want to change #selfie to #formyselfie. It's corny for sure, but it's exactly where I wish the mindset was regarding these sorts of personal expressions. There's nothing wrong with taking a picture of yourself so long as it's not done to compensate for a lack of self love or an attempt to cover up pain or real issues.

Take a selfie and place #formyselfie somewhere in the picture and post it to https://www.facebook.com/manifestingwithcathlene/ and @cathlene_miner for Instagram, #formyselfie

30 Day Self Perception Makeover - Teen Edition

So, go get your journal and let's get started!

Today, we are going to rewrite the change over statements from yesterday. Again, be sure to visualize and feel the changed over statements when you are writing them as if they are already your reality. Going forward, you'll build every day on what you wrote the day before - unless instructed otherwise.

What do you (not others) like about you?
What do you like about your facial features? You know there is something! There's at least one thing that you're grateful for every time you look at your face in the mirror. Find it and make a list. It's important for us to focus on what we, ourselves, love about us. It doesn't matter what anybody else thinks or says, because it's not their body and it's not their life.

We are all unique. Taking the time to celebrate even the smallest part of your uniqueness brings that feature to the forefront. This allows you to be grateful every time you look in the mirror. Every time you walk into a room. When you start every day off grateful for a unique part of your appearance, you raise your vibrational energy. When you raise your energy vibrations, you radiate a higher energy frequency and you open the flow for those "things" you desire to come your way.

Today's Inspired Action

Now, write about a physical feature you love on your face. It could be your nose, eyes, lips freckles, teeth, or skin. It can be anything, however small, that brings joy or a good feeling into your consciousness. If you are having a hard time with this, look back on those positive self affirmations. Positive self talk exercises are incredibly powerful and helpful. Talk and visualize.

Visualize this….Be thankful for it….Talk about it to yourself….
Really feel it!

Examples:
I love my eyes. They are the windows to my soul.
I love my freckles. They always give me a golden glow.
I love the way my eyes crinkle when I laugh. Even though I can't exactly see it, I know they are there and reflect my happiness.

> "The only cure I have ever known for fear and doubt and loneliness is an immense love of self."
> -Alison Malee
>
> -Julia
>
> (One of my favorite quotes)

Notes
for your eyes only

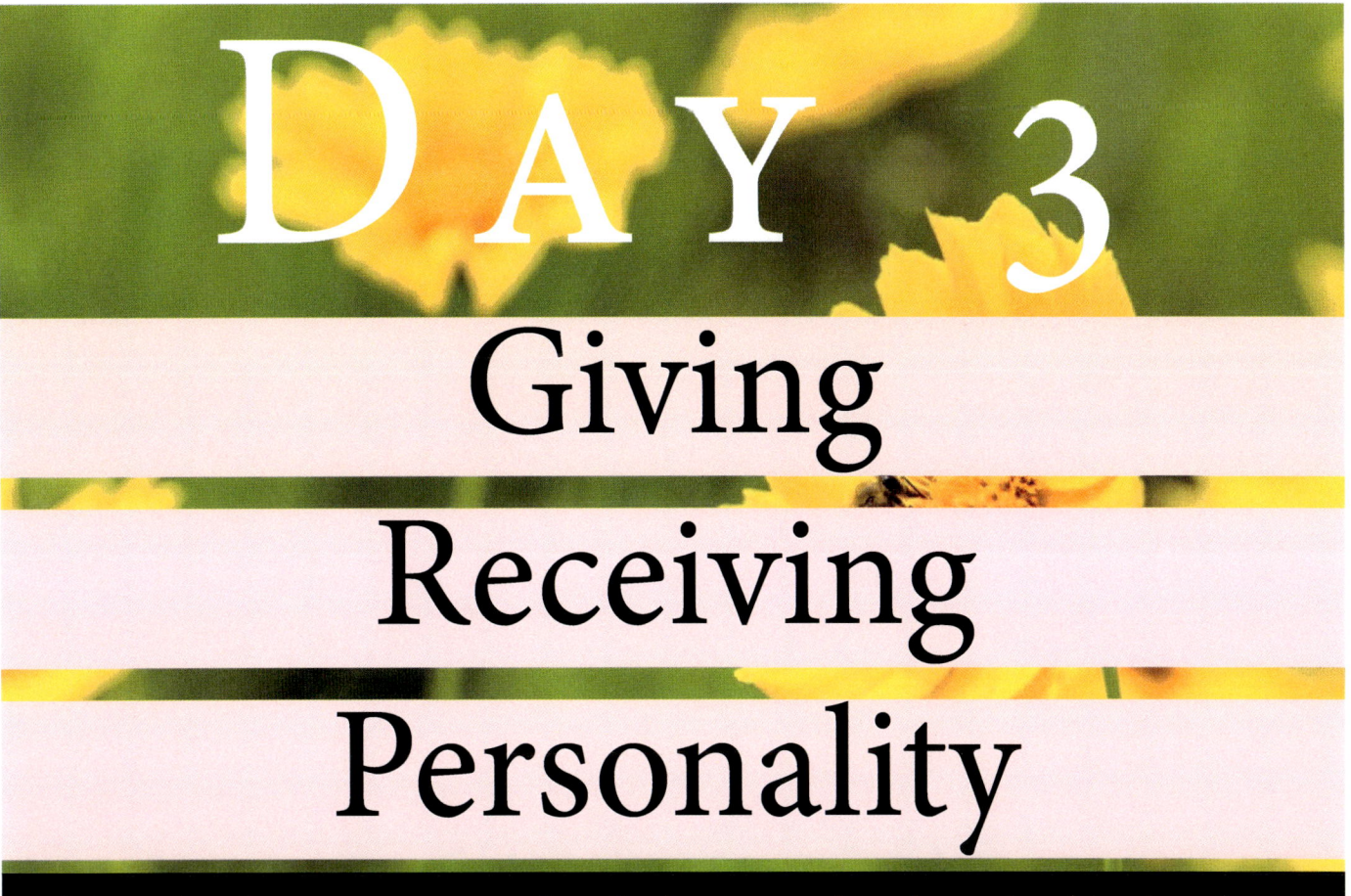

Day 3
Giving Receiving Personality

"I love that I'm a giving person. I really do give my friends, my boyfriend, and my family a lot of my time and energy. Sometimes, it really makes me feel drained and exhausted. Should relationships be this hard?"
Jessica, age 17

So, now that we have uncovered a few things to work on (we all have "things") and you have taken inspired action highlighting some great things about yourself, it's time to dive in further. Give yourself some credit on a job incredibly well done.

Keep on Going. We were all put on this earth and in this life to give and receive love. A misalignment may come when we habitually give outwardly without giving enough inwardly to ourselves. This misalignment also occurs when we do not set healthy boundaries and end up giving much more than we receive back from people that we are in relationships with.

Healthy relationships (romantic and platonic) should be balanced, have mutual respect, and bring us joy. They should be refreshing. When you are not feeling good about the way you are being treated or are feeling, like a particular relationship is unbalanced and making you feel exhausted, it's time to set boundaries and enforce them through healthy communication.

(See page 72 to read through signs of abuse and a list of resources available to you if you suspect you are a victim.)

Giving. Giving is most likely a part of your personality. Yes, it's a beautiful and admirable trait to have, but do you give too much? Do people "expect" you to give, give, and give? You must have boundaries with everything, even good things! Any great trait that we have about our personality still must have boundaries.

It's okay to say "NO." If it doesn't feel right, rethink it. Rethink it before you "over" give or "over" share. We can save ourselves from a lot of drama when we make ourselves a priority and begin setting boundaries, speaking our truth, and choosing wisely who we share private matters with.

Remember, not everyone is in alignment with you. There are still some people living more from their egos. So, you have to be the one to set the boundaries. If not, you will be left trying to pour from an empty cup – and that always leaves us overwhelmed and drained. Slow down and take care of yourself.

I know as a teenager you can sometimes feel like there is a lot of pressure to never say no, because we don't want to let anyone down. This causes unnecessary stress. Saying no and spending that extra time and energy on yourself will help you relieve that stress. It will also allow you to clear your mind so you can make better decisions overall.

It's time to turn this around so that you feel fulfilled with your loved personality trait. This allows the love that you have for yourself to radiate out to those around you with no negativity attached.

Which of your personality traits gets you feeling fulfilled and inspired? Now, really think about the role it plays in your relationships. Do you have boundaries with it? You may have to think about this for a little while, but the answer is there.

Today's Inspired Action

What do you love about your personality?

- Do you loved that you're outgoing?
- Do you love that you think of others often?
- Do you love that you are hopeful?
- Do you love that you are helpful?

Do you have the needed boundaries with it? Really think about this for a minute.

Now, write it down.

For example, I like that I am outgoing. I like that being outgoing frees me to talk to others and meet new people. This keeps me connected and growing. It also builds my confidence.

"No beauty shines brighter than that of a good heart."
-Unknown

I also know that I cannot spend a lot of time with everyone that I connect with. People come into my life for a reason and I love to connect. I will find out if I am learning from them or if they are learning from me. Are we learning from each other? All I know is that my outgoing personality allows this connection for me.

So, I like that I am outgoing.

As you write about what you love about your personality visualize yourself and this characteristic with the appropriate boundaries.

Tip: Keep in mind the reasons you started the 30 Day Self Perception Makeover anytime you question yourself on your consistency and dedication.

Remember, this is not hard! It just takes a little dedication and consistency. Anytime a negative thought comes into your head, open up your journal and re-read all of the positive things about you. Use the self-affirmations, positive self-talk, and build your self-confidence.

Notes
for your eyes only

Day 4
Becoming a Manifesting Master

"I have an idea of what I would like to be. It just seems like what I want is too big for me to achieve. There's just so much I'd like to accomplish, but I don't know how I'm going to get it all done. I know I should stay positive, but sometimes it's hard when there is so much going on for me everyday."
Dana, age 17

If you've followed along consistently and put the time in for yourself, you already see small shifts in your life. Even if you're just more aware of your thoughts and feelings and what kind of energy you are radiating out. Remember, this is about taking baby steps. Small consistent changes are far more likely to stick. We are in this for the long haul.

By staying aware of your thoughts and feelings, you have a direct map of how you radiate. This allows you to foresee what kind of "things" you will manifest in your life. This gives you a chance to change your focus and shift your day, which leads to shifting your life.

As you re-read, write, feel, and visualize what you journaled on previous days, you will get "jazzed" and excited.

This is very important as you retrain your subconscious mind. Your brain will start naturally leaning towards positive thoughts and self talk.

When you are in an energetically quiet place you feel truly connected. From here you can listen and access anything that the universe is trying to tell you. You open up your flow. Flowing is growing!

"Of this to be sure; you do not find a happy life….you make it."
-Thomas S. Monson

The "Go To Vision"

Are you ready…?

It's your "Go To Vision"….and it's oh so sweet. This is one of my favorites because it works every… single…time…It raises your energy frequency vibration at the snap of a finger.

It takes some work at first to become efficient at it – so don't get discouraged. Practice makes perfect and everyone's "Go To" is unique to them. There is no "Go To" vision in this universe like yours. It puts you on the high vibe energy frequency that attracts the same level high energy frequencies into your life. This means that you are able to attract all of that goodness faster and easier.

Using different parts of your brain while you put your "Go To Vision" into action retrains your subconscious mind. So, think of something, anything, that truly makes you smile and happy and gets you jazzed up 100% of the time.

You will be using feeling emotion and visualization for this exercise. Remember, whatever evokes that immediate happiness and excitement can be anything. Your "Go To Vision" is not something you "should" have. It is not what your parents, friends, or society define as happiness. This is all about you. If your friends and family get you jazzed 100% of the time, then YES. If not, then NO!

This is unique for everyone. It could be that you love to Jet Ski. If this is it, then visualize yourself on the Jet Ski. Feel the wind rushing by your body, feel the sun shining on your shoulders, taste the salt (or fresh) water in your mouth. Feel those exciting butterflies in your stomach as you ride over the wake.

It could be that your best friend or a parent makes you smile every time you interact. Visualize their face, feel those belly laughs, feel their hugs around your neck, and feel the safety you have with them. Find whatever you look forward to and create a mental vision board full of the mental images and movies that translate to those particular feelings.

It could be that you are standing on stage in front of a million people singing your favorite song. Visualize the audience, hear the roaring of the crowd, the applause, the whistles. Feel the heat from the lights shining on you like the star you are. Take in the smell of the equipment as the band plays behind you. Feel the joy of being adored by your fans.

This must be something that you can visualize like a scene or movie playing out in your head. It's a place and time to which you can transport instantly.

You will then immediately feel a lift in your energy frequency. Even the slightest rise in energy frequency opens your flow. It has a huge effect on your ability to manifest the life you desire.
The scene may change as you grow and time goes on and that's okay. Just be sure that you always know your "Go to Vision".

Have it at the ready and practice it. Every time you use your "Go to Vision", tell the universe that you are ready to accept the beauty that is before you and already within you.

Practice Makes Perfect

Sit quietly in a comfortable spot. Visualize and play that movie in your head of that "thing" or circumstance that makes you bubble over with excitement, your "Go To Vision". Remember, it's not the visualization itself, but the uplifting feelings it causes that are important.

FEEL it
SMELL it
TASTE it
SEE it

It's good to make sure you give yourself some personal time to meditate or to reflect each day. Stay in that space until those excited butterflies make it hard to sit still. Get so excited that you just want to shout, "Yes, yes!! I feel it, that's it!!"

That's the feeling we are shooting for. The one that changes your energy frequency vibration instantly. It takes you from a "funk" straight to a high energy vibration. It skips right over mediocre. The miracles that happen right before your eyes are nothing less than amazing. Even the so-called small ones.

Here is another place to celebrate and be grateful for, each small shift and gift that shows up in your life. Do this anytime you have a spare minute (or 18 seconds).

Today's Inspired Action

Get your journal.

As you've done on previous days, rewrite what you've written every day so far (you can paraphrase if it's time you're concerned about…this is more of a reflection and visualization and feeling exercise). Keep building on your writing. Be sure that you visualize and feel everything you write as if it's already your reality.

Now, you are going to write your "Go To Vision". When you move it from your brain onto paper, you shift and retrain your subconscious mind that much faster.

From now on this is your "Go To" way of quickly changing your energy frequency to a higher level. And, side note, your way of going from down and out to up and in it.

Every day as you write, get into "that place" and add your "Go To Vision" to your journaling.

> ### Girl, you've got good vibes!

NOTES
for your eyes only

DAY 5
Doing Every Day Right

> "I find myself constantly wondering what others think about me when I go to school. I'm always worried about how others feel, but I never really ask myself how I'm feeling. It can get really exhausting. I wish there was a way I could stop worrying so much. I just don't know how."
>
> Angela, age 16

Let's start today with a super important question and a tip to begin your day using your newly founded "Go to Vision!"

Did you check in with yourself when you got out of bed this morning? What energy frequency were you radiating out? Do you know how to tell?

Ask yourself these questions:

How do you feel mentally and physically?

- Optimistic?
- Hopeful?
- Dreading the day?
- Sick?
- Achy?

Now is when you use laser focus…get your "Go To Vision" out of your pocket (maybe your virtual pocket!) and go there. Remember it's more than just seeing it in your mind, it's allowing those positive feelings to overwhelm you.

- FEEL it.
- SMELL it.
- TASTE it.
- SEE it.

Hold it, stay in that moment for at least 18 seconds (preferably longer). Get those jazzed up juices bubbling inside. Get those great butterfly feelings in your stomach.

> "Be the energy you want to attract."
> -Unknown

Congratulations!
You just used your "Go To Vision" and shifted the start of your day. (I told you this secret is golden!) Why not head straight to the mirror and compliment yourself? You are beginning to make a lifestyle and routine out of something that not only improves your quality of life but sends you jet setting onto a path of abundance. You just raised your energy and started your day at the top vibrational frequency. Anything is possible now!

Now that you are buzzing on a high energy vibration, I have a question for you:

Do you ever ask yourself what strangers think the minute they see you? Why does it matter? How does this affect your self-perception?

Because what you think and feel about this affects how you radiate.

I would bet that if you think negatively, you're wrong. We usually don't give ourselves enough credit and automatically assume the worst of what others think of us. This is why what you think about yourself is so important. In general, what we think a stranger thinks is a reflection of what we actually think of ourselves.

When you come in contact with someone you know, or even a stranger, and your first thought is "are they judging me in some way?" or "are they looking at my messy hair (insert any judgmental statement here)?" your self-perception isn't in a good place. You're putting yourself down, which lowers your energy vibrations. This brings more of the same. You also send out negative vibrations to that person, which is not a good mix.

Let's go in a different direction. Go directly to positive action. Flash a smile. Think back to day two. Remember that facial feature that you love? Imagine that person in awe of that feature.

Using your day two feature as your go-to for what others see first in you raises your vibrations instantly. And you retrain your subconscious mind in the process. Win-Win!!

Today's Inspired Action

Get your journal.

What do you feel others think the minute they see you? Think about this and then write it down.

If it's negative, write down the complete opposite. (You'll rewrite the positive statement in your journal)

Something like:

"Others notice my beautiful white teeth when I smile from my heart."

Visualize your positive statement. Hold it for at least 18 seconds.

NOTES
for your eyes only

> "It makes me feel good to be around my friends that I have a lot in common with, we can be just us and it feels amazing!"
>
> -Carolyne

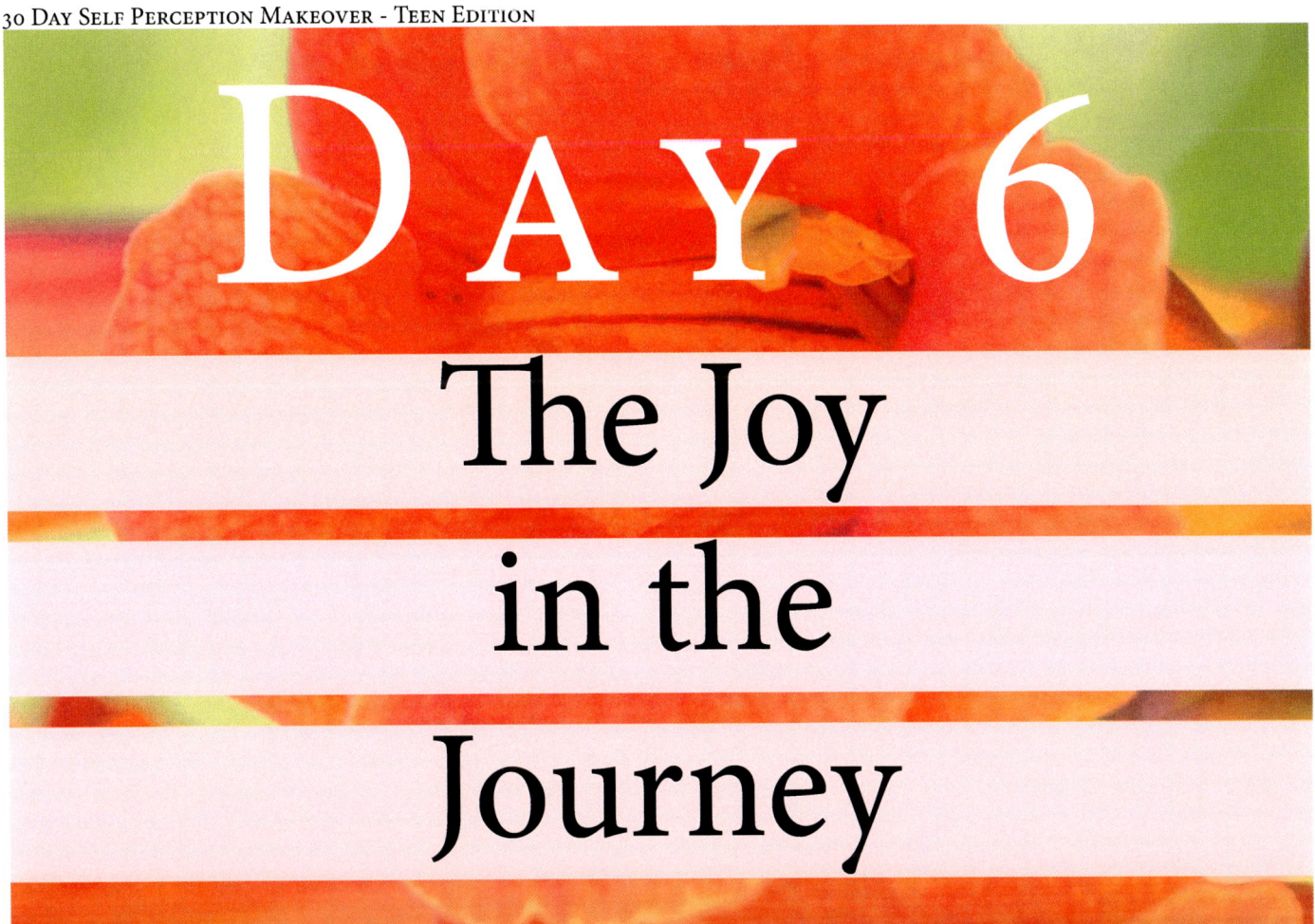

DAY 6
The Joy in the Journey

"I think one of my favorite things about highschool are my friends. They make me laugh everyday. My schedule can get really full with band practice and working after school, but I can always count on them to make me smile again. Of course, snap chat filters do the trick too.
Regina, age 15

"My dentist told me I need a crown today...I was like, I know, right?!" - Unknown

Let's talk about laughing for a minute! They always say the best medicine is laughter. Not only is it one of my favorite things to do, it also has major physical, mental health, and spiritual benefits.

Have you truly listened to you laugh?
How do you feel about your laugh?
Do you feel it is contagious?
What is the last time you truly laughed? (I mean the deep, belly laughter)
Have you ever felt embarrassed about your laugh?
Do you try and hold it in because you feel self-conscious?

Remember, just like everything else about you, your laugh is unique. It is yours and yours alone. Every time you hear yourself laugh know that you are doing something amazing for your health and wellness, physically and mentally. Maybe you don't even remember the last time you laughed. (If that is the case - we have to make a change!)

Our lives are often so serious. Some of us are juggling school, sports, family, friends, and work. On top of all of this already very demanding schedule, somehow we are supposed to also figure out what we want to do with our lives. What occupation do we want to fall into? What college do we want to attend?

Future planning has its own set of challenges.

Thoughts about failure can run rampant through our minds and consume us with self-doubt. What if we don't make our goal?

What if we don't get into the school of our choice? What if we let our family down? Maybe what you want to do with your life doesn't exactly coincide with what your parents want. The list could go on.

That's a lot for one person. Take a deep breath and acknowledge yourself and how far you've come just dealing with day to day life. It's easy to see why laughter is so hard to come by in our everyday lives sometimes.

But laughter not only raises your energy frequency vibration, it also has so many health benefits. There are numerous studies on laughter that show it releases endorphins, our feel-good chemicals, in the brain. This, in turn, helps the healing and improves how we function.

Scientific studies have proven time and time again that sick people feel better when they laugh more. Here are just a few examples:

- Laughter decreases stress hormones like cortisol and adrenaline in the body.
- Laughter brings more oxygen to your blood with the huge gulps of air it requires you to inhale.
- Laughter triggers the release of endorphins.
- Laughter improves mental functions.
- Laughter can reduce pain and speed up the healing process.
- Laughter improves cardiac health.
- And, of course, it feels good!

Add laughing to your morning routine! Yes, I am very serious here! Make it just as important as eating breakfast! Here are some suggestions to get you laughing:

> Read funny quotes on Pinterest.
> Watch funny videos or find memes that make you laugh on Instagram or Snapchat.
> Watch clips of your favorite comedian.
> Play a fun game with family or friends.
> And, laugh at yourself. Don't get mad...Laugh instead!!!

Today's Inspired Action

Get your journal!

I would like you to write down what you like about your laugh. How do you feel when you laugh? If this is not already a positive statement, it is really important to change it over.

Change it to something like: Every time I hear my laugh I know that I am opening my flow in a positive way, healing my body, and my desires are on their way.

Remember, whatever type of laugh you have, it is absolutely amazing. When you have fun and laugh from your soul you create so many health benefits for your body - not to mention, you amplify the high energy vibe you radiate out (which in turn, of course, you'll get back).

I love my laugh. It makes me feel so amazing!

> "It is time to be on this journey to better myself. There is no time better than now"
> -Cathlene Miner

Notes
for your eyes only

DAY 7
Action VS Inspired Action

> "I put a lot of pressure on myself to get into this particular college. My family really wanted me to go there, even though I was unsure it was really for me. I made sure I was involved in every activity I could get my hands on. Sports? Of course. I was so busy between studying and fulfilling these obligations I got completely burned out. When I received the letter telling me I was wait listed, I was devastated. What was all this work for?"
> Valerie, age 17

Let's touch on always being busy, busy, busy. There's action and inspired action. We must learn to tell the difference between them. Distinguishing the two will make our lives far less complicated and even open up our schedules for more time to rest and focus on ourselves.

Sometimes, you may think you need to be busy to make life better. You may even feel like staying busy is an indicator that you are moving forward, improving, or gaining traction towards your goals. You take action, action, action. However, being busy and acting for action's sake is not the same as taking inspired action.

You know the whole running around in a circle thing? Yeah, we've all been there. Knowing when you need to slow down before you get overwhelmed and exhausted is key!

When you stop before you reach that worn down point, you'll stay in the middle (mediocre) energy frequency vibration rather than dropping into the negative. But you may feel like you're stuck. You've plateaued.

Once you recognize the signs you can work on going up from there. You may feel like you're just going through the motions. You're taking action, but not inspired action.

The beauty of this is that you will begin to recognize it.

You'll stop and listen to your body. When you need rest, you'll rest. When you need a change, you will change. Honoring those simple physical promptings is the simplest way to read your own daily actions and determine whether or not they are pushing you forward or dragging you down.

Realize that always being busy can actually slow down the progress of forward movement in your life. You may have the "it has to happen faster fever" (this is your ego self kicking in here!) and it's actually counterproductive in the long run.

When you slow down, you can then resume with inspired action when it's time. You'll feel the difference between inspired action and action.

An inspired action is a feeling that comes from within. Your inspired actions have light behind them, passion, and meaning. They will actually energize you and leave you feeling satisfied. You approach those inspired actions with an open mind and it's exciting.

Action, just plain action, is the action you take because you "should" or you "have to." I understand, this is life and we sometimes have to take action on things that don't thrill us. However, even in those situations, knowing the difference can create a place of positivity.

Knowing that you do certain things because you "have to" improve a specific grade (or fill in the blank) is a stepping stone realization. You can move forward from there. Rethink the "shoulds." They may not be as necessary as you first thought. They may keep you looking at a glass half empty, which blocks and weighs you down every time.

This is another very important reason why self-perception work is key. You'll honor yourself and tune into how you feel. You'll listen to all those messages and promptings that your body gives you. You can tell whether you are taking inspired action or just plain action. And a huge part is that you will trust yourself 100%!

When the "busy, busy, busy"..." action, action, action" dance takes over you can't recognize the times you truly feel amazing doing whatever lights you up.

Today's Inspired Action

Get your journal.

Let's take a minute and think about what you're doing when you feel your best. Think about what you visualize doing that lights you up and moves you forward. If you've been in busy, busy, busy mode most of the time, you might have to dig deep. Just know those feel-good times are in there somewhere.

This could be the way you feel when you do a certain task. Perhaps it's a goal that excited you to take inspired action, even though it may be a lot of work. It could be a certain way that you feel while doing that "thing" that lights you up. By the way, keep an account of those things as you go through this process. (Write them down)

It may be a time when you allowed yourself to slow down and enjoy the scenery. Write a descriptive entry about that particular place. How does it feel? What does it look like? Close your eyes and really soak it in.

We know that moment. It's when we feel great, amazing, and hopeful. If it's not coming to you right away, it's okay! Take a few minutes for yourself in the quiet. Think about those amazing memories or places and let them come to you.

When you reflect on the ties that you feel amazing about yourself, you feel a twinge of excitement bubble up. Let it grow (glow!) from there.

Answer this question: When do you feel the best about yourself?
As you write, visualize and feel being in that moment for at least 18 seconds.

Tip to pay attention to: The next time you take action on something, what does it feel like in these 18 seconds? Inspired? Or stale, just action?

> "The kind of beauty I want most is the hard-to-get kind that comes from within - strength, courage, dignity."
> - Ruby Dee

Notes
for your eyes only

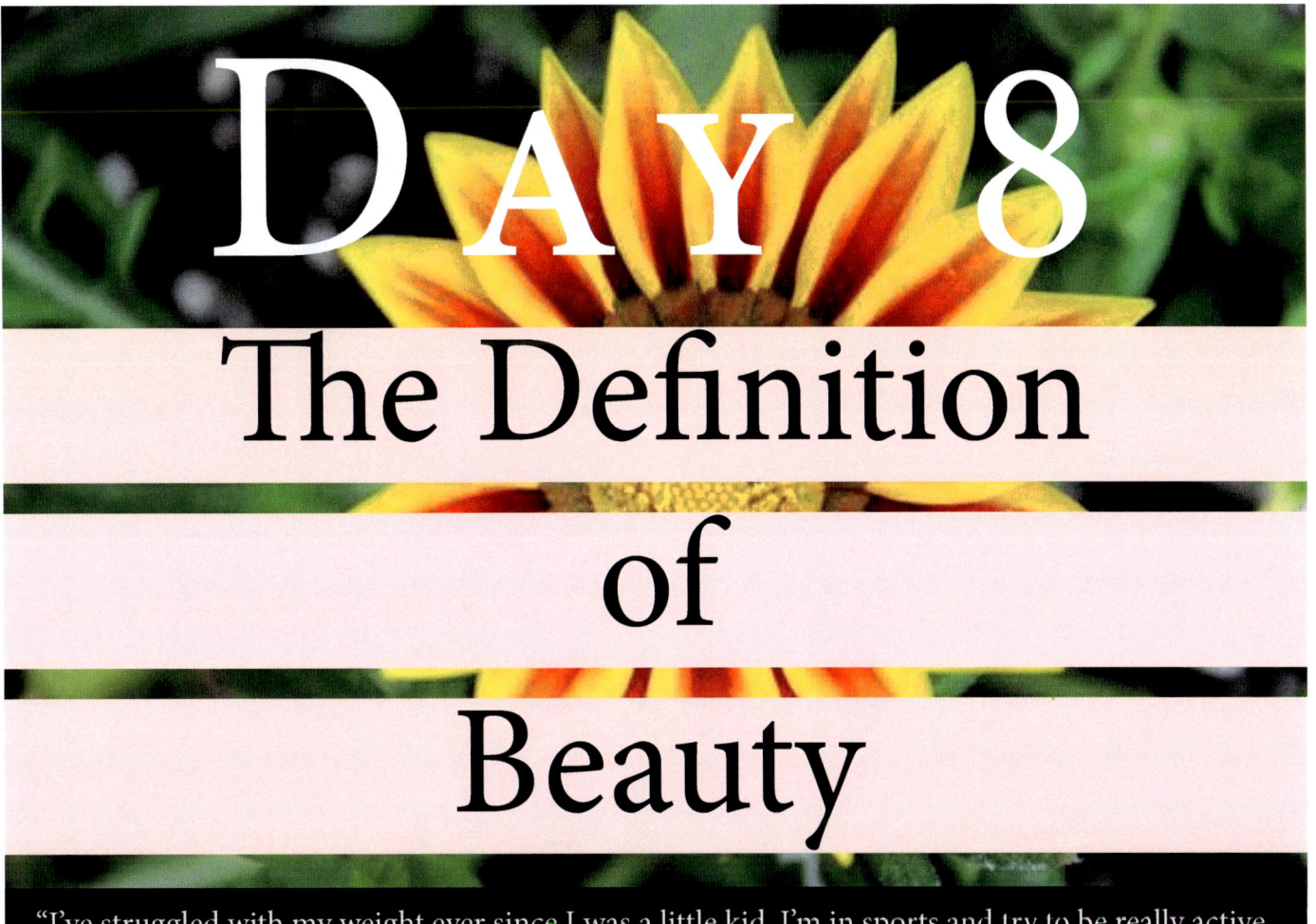

Day 8
The Definition of Beauty

> "I've struggled with my weight ever since I was a little kid. I'm in sports and try to be really active, but I've always been a little bigger than everyone else. Sometimes, I won't even go to pool parties because I'm so self conscious. My friends and family always tell me I'm beautiful, but I don't feel that way. I wish there was a magic switch I could flip in my head to make me feel differently about myself."
> Danielle, age 16

Every day you've written something new. Something that allowed you to reflect on the way that you feel, really feel, on the inside, about you.

This leads to your improved self-perception. Positive talk becomes such a habit that negative thoughts actually take work. You are creating a lifestyle in which manifesting your desires and happiness are like second nature to you. This means that things come quicker and staying on that "high vibe" cloud is easy. And oh! The changes you will see!

You'll notice that you don't judge yourself. You become your definition of beautiful. We hear about beauty all of the time. Everyone else's definition is literally shoved before our faces from social media right down to the magazines in the grocery check out line.

These days we are bombarded with images of what others think is beautiful. We allow this to override our true intuitive feelings about beauty - and we allow our ego self to step in.

When we consider the definition of beauty, it almost always includes the words "she" and "woman" and refers to physical appearance. It's no wonder society judges women on the "beauty" - as society defines it. In reality, the only thing that matters is the beauty that you see in yourself. We are all born unique and we are all "beautiful" with our own qualities. Beauty is more on the inside than the outside. Inner beauty radiates out like a glow! It's infectious and impossible to not want to be around. It's, quite literally, irresistible.

Inner beauty is felt. When you have inner beauty the

outside is already beautiful. Being beautiful is not a reflection, it is a feeling...Being beautiful radiates from your soul (something that Sam doesn't have)... So now, what is your definition of beautiful?

Today's Inspired Action

Get your journal.

What is your definition of beautiful? Not anyone else's (or society's) definition.

My definition of beauty is somebody that radiates positive energy I can feel. I truly feel their energies and see the beauty radiating from them. Beauty goes beyond what something or someone feels like. It's based on how it makes you feel.

"Beauty is not in the face; beauty is a light in the heart."
-Kahlil Gibran

NOTES
for your eyes only

_____
_____
_____
_____
_____
_____
_____
_____
_____

Day 9: You Are Limitless

"I love how I can make my friends and family happy just by being myself. Being able to do this makes me the most confident and makes me feel accomplished. The fact that I can walk into a room and people are better for it truly makes me the most fulfilled. I figure that I can do anything I want in life so long as I have this ability."
Jane, age 15

You are limitless….once you grasp and believe that (really feel it!), everything starts to change.

But, this change starts within you!

Remember your definition of beautiful? Let's think about this for a minute. Close your eyes, focus inward, and think about what you wrote on Day Eight for your definition of beautiful.
This is all about self-perception. What you think about beauty directly influences your self-perception. Beauty isn't just about your features or your weight. It is much deeper than that.

Just know, that your size, weight, or facial symmetry is perfect as is. This is something you need to repeat to yourself whenever you are feeling moments of insecurity.

It's important to look in the mirror and fall in love with yourself every day.

When you are not your definition of beauty it can show up in many ways. It may be low self-esteem, low self-confidence, or you may doubt your decisions. Maybe you allow yourself to stay in toxic relationships (that includes friendships) in which you settle for what you mistakenly think you deserve. Maybe you don't listen to your intuition (your gut instincts) because you don't trust it 100%.

Are you trying to live up to your own made-up story about beauty?

It's important to look in the mirror and fall in love with yourself every day.

When you are not your definition of beauty it can show up in many ways. It may be low self-esteem, low self-confidence, or you may doubt your decisions. Maybe you allow yourself to stay in toxic relationships (that includes friendships) in which you settle for what you mistakenly think you deserve. Maybe you don't listen to your intuition (your gut instincts) because you don't trust it 100%.

Are you trying to live up to your own made-up story about beauty?

Society has given the word "beauty" too much power. This one word…" beauty"…could affect you in ways you don't even realize. It can make you feel like you aren't capable of giving that presentation or that you can't go to that dance by yourself.

It can make you feel that the reason why someone doesn't like you is that you might be overweight or because you aren't "pretty enough." The truth is, not everyone is meant for us and that's actually a good thing. Why would we want to enter into a relationship with someone who doesn't see the absolute masterpiece we really are anyway?

Remind yourself that you are limitless. Once you begin to believe you are beautiful, you'll have the confidence to change certain things that held you back - all due to your definition of beauty. You'll start creating opportunities for yourself proactively instead of holding yourself back from them. The word "beautiful" has a lot of impact on our subconscious minds, and much of it has been put there without us even knowing it, by outside influences through the years.

You must align two ideas: your definition of beautiful and what you feel about your beauty. When you do this, space opens for amazing opportunities out there waiting for you.

If these two ideas are not aligned, you'll keep playing the less than game with yourself. You'll keep telling yourself that you don't live up to an expectation that is literally made up! Your subconscious mind keeps you believing that story. Please remember that your subconscious mind holds onto and grows stories as long as you keep feeding it.

Tell it a different story. Only you have the power to change it.

Today's Inspired Action

Get your journal.

Reflect on your definition of beautiful from Day Eight.

Do you think and feel that you are your own definition of beautiful?

My definition was: My definition of beauty is somebody that radiates positive energy I can feel. I truly feel their energies and see the beauty radiating from them.

So, I wrote: I radiate positive energy to those around me. I am beautiful.

I visualize as I write that I am truly beautiful. I am visualizing rays of light flowing from me and beaming beautiful energies to those who surround me. With exercise, I retrain my subconscious mind.

You must truly know that you are enough and that you are working towards your own personal version of success. Most importantly, you must know that you are worthy of receiving these things. If you are having trouble doing this, include the daily affirmations that are available to you in this book. Keep repeating them!

> "No beauty shines brighter than that of a good heart."
> - Unknown

Notes
for your eyes only

> I'm here to tell you that no matter what your past looks like, you are gonna get through it and come back stronger then you were going into that situation.
>
> - Haley

Day 10
Giving Compliments

> "Whenever my friends are wearing a cute outfit or achieve something great I'm always quick to compliment or praise them. I do this especially when I know they are having a bad day. I feel like girls don't do that enough for each other. Sometimes it seems like there is a silent competition or something. I don't feel that way, so I choose to be different."
> Marisol, age 16

Here is another quick way to raise your energy vibration, a tip for your bag of tricks. This one not only raises your own vibration by someone else's as well.

Compliments. Give them when you see them!

Giving a compliment raises that person's vibration and yours too! A simple compliment can shift the flow of your day and the other person's too. It's a win-win!

Why wouldn't you do something as often as possible if it spreads positive energy all around? You would, right?! It's also a practice of confidence. Sometimes, we might be afraid of putting ourselves out there even to be nice to someone. The truth is, there's nothing to be afraid of!

So, what do you think about giving compliments? Do you give out compliments often? When you do, do you look people in the eye and really make a connection?

Pay attention today. Observe how giving another person a compliment raises your own vibration - and theirs. If you're not doing this it may be because it's uncomfortable. However, practice makes you comfortable! You can even start by complimenting yourself.

Just go for it! Give a compliment. See how much better you feel! We should all live a lifestyle of building each other up. This is just one of the many ways to do it!

Today's Inspired Action

Get your journal.

Write down a compliment that you like to give. I know this can be very specific to a person, but there is usually something that we focus on.

For example, I like to compliment people's eyes. When they radiate out positive energy I see it in their eyes. I also feel it. I compliment many other areas too, but I look people in the eyes first.

If this is something that you're not used to doing, that's okay. What do you feel comfortable complimenting someone on? As you write out that compliment be sure to visualize yourself giving that compliment.

See the smile on their face. Pay attention to how they stand just a little taller and the glow that sparks in their eyes.

"Remember, life is not a competition. Give out compliments and build each other up!"
-Cathlene Miner

NOTES
for your eyes only

_____
_____
_____
_____
_____
_____
_____
_____

Day 11
Receiving Compliments

"It's really hard for me to take a compliment. I guess if I don't really feel like it's true, it's hard for me to accept it from someone else. Whenever I get a compliment I find myself feeling very uncomfortable and sluffing it off quickly. I can tell it that sometimes it hurts whoever is complimenting me. If there was a way I could accept a compliment for myself without anxiety, I would totally do it."
Shara, age 14

Did you give out compliments yesterday? Did you pay attention and feel how much you raised your vibration and that of the other person? I challenge you to keep doing this today and every day. Make a goal in the morning of how many people you plan to compliment that day.

Now, let's talk about receiving a compliment. Sometimes that can be more challenging than offering them! How do you typically receive compliments without putting yourself down? Typically, when we feel uncomfortable receiving a compliment the big "Oh, that" starts and we downplay the compliment we just received. "Oh, this shirt? It's so old…"

This is a way of putting ourselves down and not giving ourselves any extra attention, which lowers our energy frequency for sure!

You are just as deserving of compliments as anybody else. If a compliment is given with sincerity and taken with gratitude it creates such a positive energy that things happen in your life in ways that seem like magic. It puts an ease and comfort around the two people involved and fills their surroundings with light.

When we keep our energy vibration high we see shifts for the better, faster.

Keep in mind that compliments come from a place of love. Even if it's a stranger, if you feel inclined to give a compliment there is a connection made. That connection is on the receiving and the giving end of a compliment.

It reminds us that we are all made up of energy and are connected on a spiritual level in this universe. So, start by being more aware of how you receive compliments with a simple, "Thank you!" You deserve it! You are worth it. It may seem little, but it is absolutely huge!

It's time to pay attention and think about the compliments that you like to receive and give. It's such a great feeling!

Today's Inspired Action

Get your journal.

Write down the compliment that you love to receive! Maybe there is more than one. Write all of them down. Remember to visualize yourself receiving these compliments with a simple confident, "Thank you."

Every time you graciously and openly receive, you raise your energy vibration and, in tandem, that of the person doing the complimenting!

"Talk to yourself like you would to someone you love."
-Brene Brown

NOTES
for your eyes only

_____
_____
_____
_____
_____
_____
_____
_____

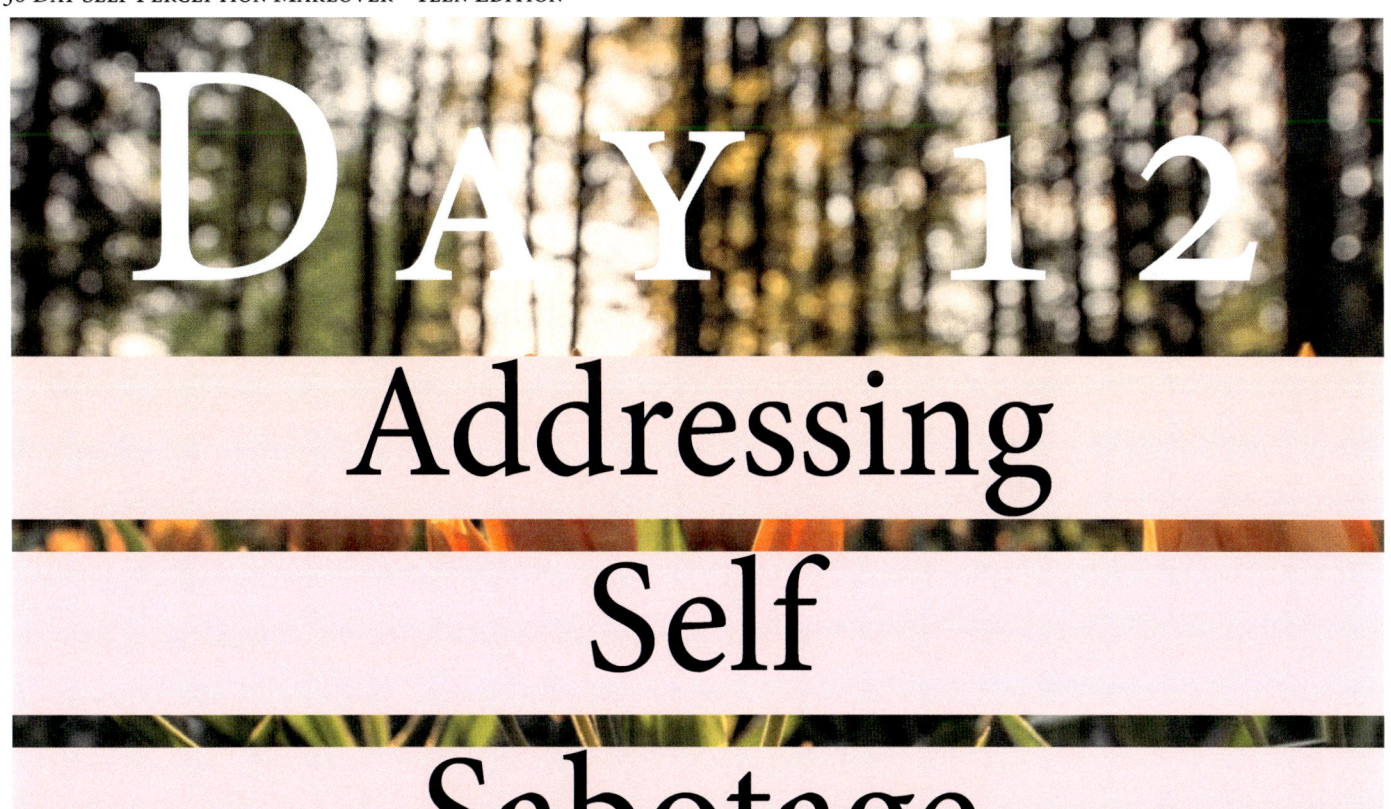

DAY 12
Addressing Self Sabotage

"It's hard for me to change habits when I don't really know which ones are setting me back. Sometimes, I think it might be sleeping in a little too often. However, my schedule drains me so much that I need the sleep. How do I know what activities to cut out when all of them seem so vital to my success?"
Ashley, age 17

Let's take a look at your self-sabotaging habits…

Self sabotaging habits hold you back from your desires. What do you do on a regular basis that you feel keeps you from the success that you desire?

This is a negative pattern, that becomes a habit, and begins a cycle of self-sabotage. By becoming aware of your self-sabotaging habits, you bring some limiting beliefs and blocks to the surface. The great thing about habits is that they are never permanent. You can always turn the boat around and create new ones. Helpful habits that allow growth.

It's time to pinpoint them and call them out.

• •

Possible self-sabotaging habits could be:

- Perfectionism (nothing is ever good enough)
- Do you always procrastinate?
- Maybe you put off doing things for yourself.
- Putting off getting healthier until "tomorrow."
- Waiting to start a project until you have more time.
- You are always reinventing the wheel instead of moving forward.
- You're always "too busy" to move forward.

Maybe insecurity keeps you quiet when your opinion would be valued and important. It could be that you skip breakfast every day and run out of energy by mid-morning. It could even be that you're spending too much time with your friends and not putting

putting needed focus into your family. Maybe you exercise too much or too little.

It's time to take inspired action!

Remember, inspired action is different than just action. It's that flame inside that's ready and motivated! It says now is the time! You take inspired action to break those cycles that block you from your version of success.

Today, we flip these into something positive. A positive action stops the cycle! Remember, when you journal, that you must visualize and get into that feeling place. Don't be discouraged if that not so good habit doesn't dissolve right away. We don't move forward by looking backwards. It may take several attempts to rid yourself of those self sabotaging habits. The important thing is, you're doing it!

We are flipping that habit! That one that is holding you back!

Tips to Kick Self-Sabotage

Get your journal.

Is there a positive action or a healthier alternative that you can put in the place of your self-sabotaging habit? Is there anything you can avoid or stay away from that may trigger yours?

> "You cannot have a positive light and a negative mind."
> -Joyce Meyer

Picture what a situation (or day) would look like if you did not have that self-sabotaging habit.

What would that day feel like?
What would it look like?
What would you accomplish?
How would this change your life long term?

When you put this into practice, you are on the way to kicking your self-sabotaging habit. And that much closer to the changes you've been waiting on. The changes that will direct you toward your unique fulfilling path.

While you write these self-sabotaging habits down, be sure that you are coming from a place of love. Do not feel bad about yourself or judge yourself harshly while you think about them. Everybody has faced their self sabotage at some point in their lives. The difference now and the amazing thing is that you are acknowledging them. You are bold and brave enough to face them and change them. Not many people do.

Let's think about getting over the hurdle of self-sabotage!

Notes
for your eyes only

"A big part of the way you see yourself is the people you surround yourself with and how they influence your perception. Make sure they're positive! If people in your life aren't benefiting you and your health you don't need them!"
-Emercyn

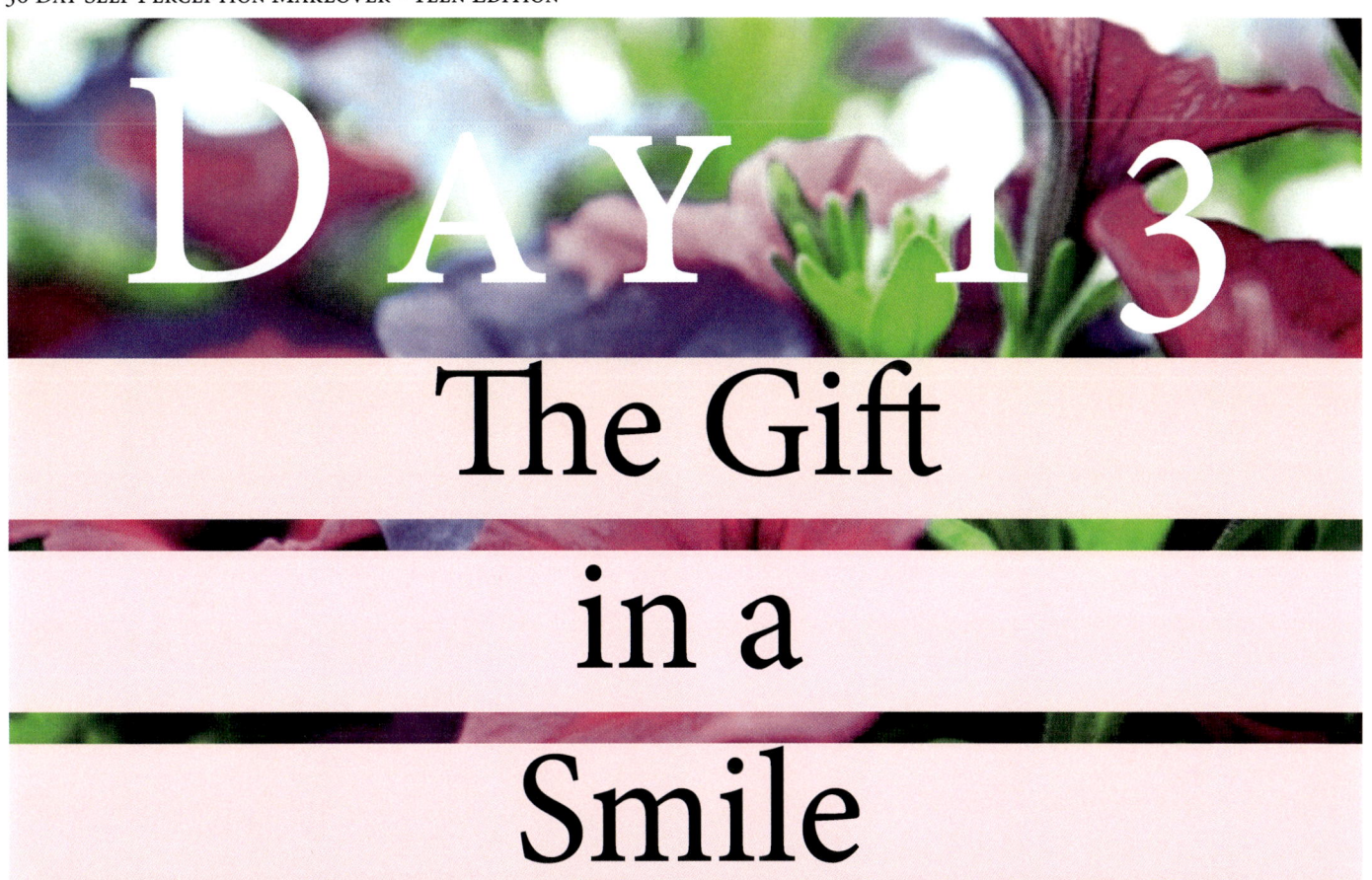

Day 13
The Gift in a Smile

"I smile as much as I can! I think it should be something I do more. I have great friends and family, but it can be hard to maintain an attitude where all you do is smile when there is so much pressure on a daily basis. Sometimes, it's hard to 'smile through it.'"
Jessica, age 13

Today is full of fun!!

Oh, that smile! That beautiful smile! What do you think of your smile? You may be thinking, that's a silly question. However, it's actually really important.

It doesn't have anything to do with what you think of your smile when you look in the mirror, but has everything to do with how you feel when you smile.

What is that feeling that starts bubbling up inside? What is that feeling you feel when you radiate your smile out into the universe?

Now, if you have not smiled in awhile, then right now put a smile on your face. It doesn't matter how silly it may feel.

Hold that smile for 18 seconds.

While you do this smiling exercise, go to your Go To Vision. Feel and visualize being in your Go To Vision. Remember, if you picked your true Go To Vision, it will make you smile and get jazzed 100% of the time.

Now, how do you feel? Notice the shift in how you feel. It can be very small. It can be on a molecular level throughout the cells in your body.

But something is definitely changing. Do it again if you need to. If you have to force a smile, you may feel silly or annoyed. It's ok, I promise you are raising your energy vibrations even if it's just a twinge. It's a start!

Numerous studies show that a smile using the muscles at the corner of your mouth (zygomaticus major) and the muscles that close your eyes (orbicularis oculi) trigger your brain to release endorphins.

You just realized you need to smile more!

Today's Inspired Action

Get your journal.

Today, write in your journal how your smile makes you feel. Write a reminder of how your smile lifts your spirits and retrains your subconscious mind. You might also want to include how you think your smile affects others as well. A smile from you makes others smile and reminds them that they are "seen." You never know what is going on in a person's life, and a smile can help them and literally change their day or their life.

If you're not sure, flash a smile at a stranger and pay attention to how you feel.

Start by saying, "hello." That way your mouth is already in motion. The smile then comes naturally. While you are smiling, take a mental note of how you feel right that very second. Look in the mirror and flash yourself a smile.

Everyday challenge: Smile at someone at least once a day.

> "Everything is created twice. First in the mind and then in reality."
> -Robin S. Sharma

Notes
for your eyes only

NOTES
for your eyes only

Day 14

The Letter

"Writing my letter to the universe was so liberating. It filled me with peace and hope. I guess it taught me to give myself permission to believe that everything was possible. Like writing a letter to someone who genuinely cares and wants to help. I found myself dreaming so much bigger and with more confidence after I wrote mine."
Abigail, age 15

So, today is totally different.

Today, you'll write a letter to the universe, God, or whatever resonates most with you. You'll write a letter about what you are most grateful for about you.

Really get specific with this letter! You won't rewrite this letter every single day. So, go all out and let it be as long and detailed as it needs to be.

Now, there is no negativity or negative self talk allowed. This is all about what you are grateful for as it relates to you. By focusing on just you and your life right now, you bring things to the surface that you may not think of often.

These are such inspiring and refreshing thoughts.

Write your letter to the universe. Be specific. Read it as often as you need to. When you have a down day, go back and reread your letter. Remind yourself why you are so grateful to be here in this amazing life.

> "You must master a new way to think before you can master a new way to be."
> -Marianne Williamson

Notes
for your eyes only

DAY 15
The Habits that Move You Forward

> "It sounds kind of funny, but the best habit I have is making my bed every morning. Sure, there are others I possess that might sound better. However, when I make my bed every morning it's like I'm starting the day on the right foot. I feel like everything kind of falls into place if I do that first."
> Marianne, age 17

How did you do with writing your letter to the universe? I loved writing mine. It was like a weight was lifted.

We are reminded of how amazing we are. Most importantly, we are actually doing it for ourselves.

It is hard for me to believe that we are already halfway through this 30 Day Self Perception Makeover! You're seeing big shifts and noticing differences in the way you feel about yourself.

You'll notice that the things coming into your life are more in line with the high energy vibration that you are on! You feel a more glass half full mentality most of the time. Remember, it's a lifestyle we are creating.

Today, we touch on habits that keep us moving forward everyday. These are the opposite of our self-sabotaging habits. These we celebrate and honor ourselves for. We all have habits! Some of them move us forward and others keep us stuck.

Which ones keep you moving forward? What habit, or habits, contribute to your success?
You have some I am sure!!

Writing them down, and connecting with them, helps us know that we are heading in the right direction. We follow our intuition and take inspired action. It keeps us grateful for the habits that are getting us there and reaffirming their importance in our subconscious minds.

You already listed the self-sabotaging habits to be changed over, but what do you do on an everyday basis that moves you in the direction you desire?

Do you wake up at the same time every day and take inspired action toward your desires?

Do you exercise routinely?

Do you go to bed at a decent time to get enough sleep?

Do you journal?

Do you meditate or pray regularly?

These are great habits. These great habits are why amazing changes happen in your life! Changes, big and small, in the direction of your desires are exciting. It's also nice to celebrate our wins (something you should do everyday).

Be sure to celebrate and be grateful for each one of them. Look and see how far you have come.

Now, yours may not be on the list I gave, but you have them! The evidence is in the very air you are breathing. You're alive!

Today's Inspired Action

Get your journal.

Which of your current habits contribute to your success?

Write them down. This helps you remember that you are headed in the right direction. It also helps you continue to take inspired action every day toward your desired life.

> "Motivation gets you going, and habits get you there."
> -Zig Ziglar

Notes
for your eyes only

> Going through my years in high school, I've learned that if we stay true to ourselves people will be more attracted to our personality! They will want to be your friend and be near you because of your positive attitude! Also, life is short! Live it up girl!! God blesses us every day and if we do what's right you will improve mentally and spiritually! That's an amazing thing! LOVE WHO YOU ARE!!!!
> -Kate

Day 16

Feeling Your Best

"I absolutely love dress shopping. Whenever there is a dance coming up, I kind of bubble up inside. I might not like the way I look in blue jeans sometimes, but I always feel great in a new dress. A dance is basically an excuse for me to feel dynamite with my friends."
Nicole, age 16

Yesterday was all about recognizing the habits that contribute to your success. You should feel good about that and also good about yourself as well!

Today, let's think about something we all do in everyday life. We all have to get dressed, right? Well, we don't have to get dressed, but walking around naked could get us put away!

Some pieces of clothing make us feel amazing while others make us feel less than our best. It might even be a uniform we have to wear for those of us in private schools. Paying attention to how we feel when wearing certain outfits makes a huge difference in how we radiate our energy.

Today, I want you to think about an outfit that makes you feel absolutely amazing! We all have an outfit that makes us feel better every time we slip it on.

We look in the mirror and are like, "YES!"

Now, it's worth mentioning here that the outfit you wear everyday may not be "the" outfit. Sometimes, we have go to outfits that makes us feel comfortable but not necessarily amazing.

Why is this important and how does this change our self perception? Because in day to day life we put the same type of clothes on. We typically do this out of ease and the desire to feel comfortable. To be clear, there is nothing wrong with comfort! Sometimes it feels amazing to be comfortable.

However, let's make sure we aren't sticking with sweats because we feel terrible about ourselves and don't want to be seen. We wear them because that's what we feel most comfortable - and amazing - in today. This is about breaking out of that "less than" mentality and wearing the clothes that resonate with the highest opinion of ourselves in the moment.

If we never take the time to make ourselves feel amazing, we aren't operating on as high a frequency as we could. Sometimes amazing means sweats. Sometimes amazing means that little black dress. Amazing never means hiding ourselves because we are afraid of the opinion of someone else or even ourselves.

When we remember how we feel in those special outfits that show off what we like best about ourselves, we take small steps towards loving every inch of our beautiful bodies. By practicing this, you will begin to feel great in every outfit. Not because of the outfit itself, but because of the brilliant being that fills it…You.

When you feel the "I rock this" outfit feeling you radiate out at a higher energy vibration. By the end of these exercises, I want you to feel that "I rock this" outfit feeling in everything you wear.

So, since we are still in the beginning stage of this makeover, I want you to think of that outfit or article of clothing that makes you feel amazing.

Why not go put in on and feel how great it is?

Today's Inspired Action

Get your journal.

What outfit makes you feel amazing? Visualize and feel yourself in it. It can be something that you wear to bed, to the gym, or out on the town. Really anything that makes you feel your absolute best!

For me, it is my white jumper with heels. It makes me feel like a movie star! I feel put together! I feel in shape!

> "The secret to great style is to feel good in what you wear."
> -Ines de la Fressange

Notes
for your eyes only

> I feel like nowadays we get too involved with all the negativity in this world. For example, social media. Social media should be a place for influencing and spreading positivity. However, I've noticed from past experience and seeing others that we tend to use it in a negative light. For instance, we are in a constant battle with ourselves and others trying to compare to one another and competing to see who can get the most likes on a post. As a result, we begin to lose who we are and forget what truly makes us happy. It's time to create our own sunshine.
> -Kaylee

Day 17
Ego Self VS Inuitive Self

"My mom talks to me a lot about 'trusting my gut' instincts. Like, sometimes I get weird feelings around some people or about decisions being right or wrong for me. It's just hard to trust that when I feel like my head talks me out of trusting it sometimes. Then it makes you question the difference. How do you know how to decipher the two?"
Emilia, age 15

Today, let's chat about your ego-self versus that of your Intuitive self.

Do you know the difference? Let's cover a few basics about your Intuitive self and your ego self.

Your ego self is best defined as that feeling you get when you are trying to be better than something or someone else, trying to "impress", or not disappoint. You ego self causes you to react to life instead of create your life. Insecurity drives us to live life from the outside in instead of the inside out. It feels like there is a rush or urgency. Like, if you do not do this right now, you will miss out. #FOMO

Your ego self is the part of you that holds a grudge or ends a relationship prematurely to save itself from possible rejection.

Limiting beliefs and blocks are derived from your ego self too (remember those made up stories in our head?).

Your ego self usually is a feeling of urgency. It tends to feel a little bit uncomfortable or anxious. You might have sort of an uneasy feeling about something but ego self will override that feeling and tell you that it's okay. If you have to do mental flips to rationalize a gut instinct, it's your ego, and usually a dead end. You'll regret it. A good friend of mine always says, "If it's light, it's right."

No heaviness for us anymore!

We recognize our ego, thank it for the input and go with our Intuition. These motivating factors all come from the external factors around us.

Something outside of your inner compass influences you to feel this way. Something good comes out of it though. You get to learn a lesson. Everything, even what appears to be terrible, is a lesson to learn. It is your mindset, belief in yourself, and confidence in goodness that determines how.

Now, just to be clear, I am not talking about things that happen to other people. You do not have control over others. Nor should you ever seek to have control. I am also not talking about the uneasy feeling you may get when you are excited and trying something new. It is also not that excited, a little bit uncomfortable feeling you get when you feel happy butterflies in your stomach. Once you begin to pinpoint where those feelings are coming from and understand the difference between your Intuitive self and ego self, you will better differentiate those butterflies to take inspired action.

Now, your Intuitive self is the part of you that makes calm decisions. Or excited decisions that feel right. It comes from a place of love. It can be compared to the little voice in your head or a gut instinct. Your Intuitive self usually has a quick answer. It is typical for people to second guess their Intuition (gut). You must trust this little voice so those big things can happen for you. It is our inner gps.

This is where the sayings "trust your gut" or "go with your intuition" come from. From here, you find answers that align with your present self, and also your future self! Sometimes, these promptings make no sense in the present. However, this inner guidance is your wisest and most loyal companion.

Your Intuitive self is that which always knows the "right" thing for you. It is always aligned with you path. It knows who you are and what you came to this existence to accomplish. It knows what you truly need beyond the narrow scope of your temporary, external circumstances.

Secret Manifesting Tip

How do you tune into your Intuitive self?

If you are new to tuning into your Intuitive self, try this... first be silent. Go to a spot where you are alone with no distractions. Even if it's just for five minutes. You might want to use things that relax you. Maybe light a candle or surround yourself with comforting things.

Sit quietly. You can call it mediation or you can call it prayers, whatever resonates with you. Clear your mind and just listen. Concentrate on your breath.

When a distraction comes to mind like, "what are you eating for lunch," let it flow by and wait for a message. It may be about something that you have been contemplating or it may be a new idea. Write it down and elaborate on it later.

If you are like me and at first have a hard time sitting quietly, try humming softly (you may have heard of the "om" exercise in yoga practices), or any other vibrating mantra that resonates with you. This occupies your subconscious mind so you can allow messages to come naturally.

It's important to practice this daily, best in the morning, so you can quickly recognize your intuitive self. Practice exercising your intuition daily. Getting better at tapping into your intuition is like anything else in life. It takes training and practice to get better. Once you know what you're listening for, you'll be a pro at recognizing it on the fly throughout the day.

It is important to know the difference between that which is instigated by external factors, that are usually based in fear, and your intuitive self. Pay attention, trust yourself, and most importantly, listen to it. Act upon it with confidence.

So, are your desires yours (intuitive self), or someone else's that you have a need to please (ego self)?

Today's Inspired Action

Get your journal.

For day seventeen, write down what that little voice says to you. Which voice runs around in your mind more often throughout the day? Which little voice comes to your mind more frequently than not?

Is it your ego self or is it your Intuitive self? Remember, our ego self comes from our made up stories. Our Intuitive self offers messages from our intuition. They come from love not from a place of insecurity or pain.

At times, we get thoughts in our mind from our ego. These are, at times, just bad habits or limiting beliefs. Knowing this, it's ideal for our intuitive self to be the main voice running around in our heads! This is the voice that it's best to take messages from and listen to. If you are someone that feels like you don't have a little voice running around in your head throughout the day, think about it, be quiet, and see what comes to mind.

If you like what the little voice reminds you of throughout the day, write it down. Maybe it is how great you are, maybe it is that money is coming to you from expected or unexpected places. What is it telling you every day? If it is telling you that you're fat or not good enough, then that is not a good voice - and is your ego self.

If it is ego self and negative, change over that statement. Go to the video https://www.cathleneminer.com/30day for instruction on how to change over statements. You must retrain your subconscious mind. Changing over statements starts that process.

Now trust the process. Really put your trust in the process. Visualize yourself in the position of that changed over statement.

> No one has learned the meaning of life until he has surrendered his ego to the service of his fellow man.
> -Beron Wolfe

NOTES
for your eyes only

_____
_____
_____
_____
_____
_____
_____
_____

Day 18
Your Body Image

> "It's not like I'm totally unhappy with the way that I look. I still go to the beach with my friends and I can hang out at the pool without being too self conscious. I've noticed that I'm constantly comparing myself with other people though. Sometimes, I'll even skip meals because I think I can look better or do better. It's kind of a cycle of being happy with myself and not."
> Dana, age 16

Today is a very important day to focus on. You might even want to revisit this day more than the others in the future. Positive body image is such a huge struggle for some teenagers and it's imperative to our self perceptions. How we feel about our bodies impacts how we feel about ourselves.

Yesterday, we recognized the little voices in your head (make friends with that positive ally) and whether they're rooted in your ego self or Intuitive self. When you know where you get your information internally it has a big effect on your self perception. It also ushers in a kind and loving voice.

Since these little voices speak to us all of the time, nurturing and training our intuitive gifts is very important. When you differentiate between your ego self and your Intuitive self, you can control other areas of your life like anxiety, depression, panic attacks, etc. All of these are by-products of feeling as if things are out of control and cannot be changed. We know now that we are in control and we can change anything we want to.

Your ego self could be a big contributor to common ailments! Your ego self is the one that makes you feel less than, not beautiful, makes you feel as if you need to be better than, or fuels anxiety. It can also make you feel as if there needs to be immediate action or you might miss out.

Most people are pleasers by nature. They desire to see others happy and will usually run themselves into the ground to make it happen.

While pleasing others has its good points, people pleasing and perfectionism come from your ego self. Even if you think you're a perfectionist for "you" and no one else, that urge is a story your subconscious mind tells you.

"I have to be perfect because (fill in the blank)."

This is why it is very important to be able to tell the difference between your Intuitive self and your ego self. You'll notice that anxiety, panic attacks, and feelings of worry show themselves less often. You'll notice that it's easier to get into a positive space when you are thinking about your body or your abilities. To get your ego self to take a back seat, you simply need to acknowledge it and call it out.

Remember, when you catch your thoughts before 18 seconds, you retrain your subconscious mind to listen to your Intuitive self, your intuition.

We've talked about self perception and how we perceive ourselves on a mental and feelings level. Now, we'll bring some parts of our body along the journey. Some you will feel this is easy, others will have to think about it. You may have to change over feelings.

Remember, when you catch your thoughts before 18 seconds, you retrain your subconscious mind to listen to your Intuitive self, your intuition.

We've talked about self perception and how we perceive ourselves on a mental and feelings level. Now, we'll bring some parts of our body along the journey. Some you will feel this is easy, others will have to think about it. You may have to change over feelings.

What do you think about the different parts of your body (legs, arms, stomach, etc…)? Is there one that you just do not love right now?

It sounds simple, but to some of us, this is a huge issue. That's okay! We all have to start somewhere.

I've found, while coaching women for over 26 years, that most of us believe that there is something wrong with at least one part of our bodies. I've also found that most of those body image issues began around adolescence and developed further into teenage years.

We know that even though somebody else could say it is absolutely perfect, it still doesn't change how we feel about it personally. It is what you think and feel that matters at the end of the day. Somebody else should not and does not have control over what you think about yourself. There is freedom in that!

Let's take some time and think about that one part (or those multiple parts) of ourselves that we don't particularly care for. Let's start the journey of recognizing that we are all perfect in our own ways.

> "The skin you are in is beautiful. You do not have to be lighter. You do not have to be darker. You do not have to lose your scars. You do not have to hide your stretch marks. You do not need make-up unless you like it. There is no addendum or asterisk to this statement. The skin you are in is beautiful. Period. End of."
> -Nita Gill, The Skin You Are In

Nobody else probably notices our perceived imperfections, except us. But what we think matters because it affects our energy frequency levels. It's our desires that are impacted.

So, let's nip this one now. We must pay attention to our thoughts and be consistent as we change over what we think about our bodies. We must think very highly of our bodies. After all, they house our souls.

Personally, I have very muscular legs. I grew up thinking that they were too big. I always felt very uncomfortable.

I had to work on this for years until I finally absolutely loved my legs. They get me everywhere I desire to go! I am not that tall and my legs can get me from point A to point B quickly! I am now grateful for my beautiful legs.

Now, think about the body part(s) that might bother you. If there are multiple areas of your body, think about them one by one. What has that individual body part done for you? Gratitude raises your energy vibration immediately!

Close your eyes and visualize yourself in your mind. Surround yourself with light and think about each one of the body parts you have been critical of. Spend time loving your body and allowing yourself to feel as beautiful as you truly are. This takes practice, but practice makes perfect in your eyes. The goal is to immediately go to positive space when it comes to your self image. So much so, that negativity takes work.

Remember, we must love each part of our body. Let's not ignore these parts. Think about the great things different parts of our bodies do for us.

I would also like to offer resources to you in the event you are struggling with an eating disorder or severe body image issue. Sometimes, we may suffer from body dysmorphic disorder or an eating disorder (usually they go hand in hand). Please visit the back of this book to locate signs you may have these issues and to get resources that will help you overcome them.

If this is an issue for you, you are not alone. I too have suffered and have successfully overcome eating disorders. I am here for you.

Today's Inspired Action

Get your journal.

Write down what you think and feel about the certain parts of your body (legs, arms, stomach, etc…). Journal about each one individually.

This is very important.

If it is a negative feeling and thought, change it over right away. Write down your changed over statement.

Have this thought (your changed over statement) at the ready in your brain. Everytime you think negatively about that body part, go to this statement and either say it out loud or think it repetitiously. Remember the visualization practice we discussed. Surround yourself in light.

Think about what that bothersome part of your body has done for you in your life. Remember how we spoke about being grateful? Be grateful for the part of your body that normally makes you say: "Aghhhh!"

P.S. If you love every part of your body then you're ahead of a lot of people. Write down a body part that you are grateful for and what it does for you.

Photo By: Carly Casella

Notes
for your eyes only

DAY 19

Your Posture

"I find it hard to sit up straight or pay attention to how I'm walking everyday. I'm in sports pretty much the whole school year and that takes a lot out of me physically. Sometimes, sitting in my desk is the only rest I feel like a really have. So, I'll slouch over and put my chin in my hand and rest on my elbow. It's not the greatest way to relax, but it works for me. I mean, why stop?"
Jessie, age 17

How do you feel so far? How did yesterday go? Did you come up with a positive statement about part of your body that you felt negatively about before? Maybe you've already used that statement today!

Doesn't it feel great to know and believe how great we really are?

Now, we add onto our body discussion. What do you think of your posture? Yes, your posture! It's been shown that standing and sitting up straight (having good posture), raises your energy vibrations immediately. It's also not something that most of us pay attention or draw their awareness to.

Why not? It's one of the easiest ways to amplify your high energy vibe!

So, right now, pay attention to your posture.

Are you in alignment?
Do you feel like you are slouching?

If so, stand or sit up straight. Pay attention to your posture throughout the day. Sitting is a time that we usually forget about our alignment. This is especially true during the school year when we probably spend more time sitting than we do standing! So, be sure to sit up straight!

It's such a simple thing to do everyday (that we normally don't think about) that helps us improve our self perception and raise our vibrations. Isn't that really cool? You open the flow to your desires just by paying attention to your posture.

Today's Inspired Action

Get your journal.

Write down the words below and visualize yourself sitting up straight at your desk or walking tall, with your head held high. Feel how confident you feel and how the energy shifts positively wherever you walk. Feel how straight your back is, feel how rolling your shoulders up and back takes some of the pressure that may cause your neck or head to ache.

Write: I love my posture (if you do).

Or, if you don't, write something like: I now stand up straight, I am proud and confident.

You will now pay attention to your posture!

Word this however feels right to you. Visualize and see how nicely your clothes lay on your body when you have great posture. Feel how open your heart is to receive the amazing things that are coming into your life.

Tip: If you feel that your posture is something that you really need to work on, set an alarm on your phone for every hour or two as a reminder to check on your posture. Pay attention to your posture. Take an extra step and tune into your feelings when the alarm goes off. How are you radiating your energy right then??

It is a small thing with a huge benefit!

"Be a pineapple - Stand tall, wear a crown, and be sweet."
—Unknown

Notes
for your eyes only

Day 20

What You Love About You

"I actually really love who I am for the most part. I do sometimes feel like I come up short. Some of my friends are so outgoing and funny. They make everyone laugh. I feel like I'm really quiet and soft spoken. I'm really good to talk to though and I'm a great listener."
Jamie, age 15

How's your posture since yesterday? You're paying more attention to it now, aren't you? Always keep in mind that this is an easy way to raise your energy vibrations. It's also a practice of confidence and confidence is key! It's easy, so be sure to do it often.

Today is sort of an easy one, but it can make a huge impact! What are those things that you love about you? It can be anything! Something about your body, your personality, or maybe even a habit you have, like getting enough exercise.

We all have at least one thing we admire about ourselves. Even if it is just one thing, it makes a big difference when we focus on it. Some days we may think differently, but that is what these 30 days are all about, isn't it? Shifting self perception?

Some people love their smile. Some people love that they are optimistic. Perhaps you love how kind and generous you are.

Personally, I love that I am outgoing! It has opened many door of opportunity and has allowed me to meet some wonderful people.

> "Remain committed to success, be loyal to your dreams, it is okay to choose yourself."
> -R.H. Sin

Today's Inspired Action

Get your journal.

What do you love about you? What is a unique gift that you possess and love?

Visualize this as you write!

So, for me (as I write this) I imagine that I am doing something and am somewhere where I am outgoing. I visualize that I am speaking to an audience of people! It raises my energy vibrations and gets me smiling!

NOTES
for your eyes only

_____
_____
_____
_____
_____
_____
_____
_____
_____
_____
_____
_____

DAY 21
What If?

> "I'm a daydreamer. My town is really small and I feel like I'm about to explode most of the time. I want to do so much in my life. I'm constantly reading books and buying magazines about travelling. It's hard being like that here sometimes, because I worry it might not happen."
> Shea, age 17

Today, we play a mind game. It's a little story. Remember the Go to Vision we had on Day 3? That something that makes you smile 100% all of the time and lights you up?! This game starts Manifesting Magic and gets you thinking about what your best life will look like. This is especially important to do at this point in your life when so many of your decisions are about the path you are about to take in life.

Go to that Go to Vision smile, visualize and get into that feeling place. We'll learn to further train our subconscious mind through this playful exercise.

Once you are in that feeling place of your Go to Vision, think about a "What If" Statement?

What if (write down something that you desire).

For Example:

What if I had a house on the water?
What if I could travel the world?
What if I got into that college?
What if I could study abroad?
What if I lived in the mountains?

Ask any "what if" that gets you all jazzed and excited! Visualize and feel yourself as if that "what if" already is here. Like you are already living it and experiencing it. Now get into that feeling place.

Okay, now that you are there, hold onto that feeling. Hold onto it and continue to visualize it.

Now we go back in time!

Go back to a time where you felt absolutely amazing! It could be when you were out of the field playing a sport and the excitement of the crowd made you feel amazing. It could even be a childhood memory. Perhaps it's the trip to Disney World and you loved the thrill of the rides.

Maybe you were on stage during a spelling bee and you spelled a challenging word right! It could be all of the times you hang out with your best friend. Maybe you were in the kitchen with your mom baking, and you felt so full and loved. Think of anything that gets you back to that feeling place.

Let's get that feeling back and start living it everyday and in every moment!

You will now go back and forth between the "what if" and the "back then" feeling.

It could be you are immersed in the feeling of being on the playing field with the lights shining down and the crowd roaring. You then switch over to a statement like: What if I was studying abroad and was enjoying different cultures and meeting interesting people?

Flip back and forth between those two feelings. You'll get all jazzed up and throw open the gates for your desires to come flooding in! It is key during this time not to worry about how these desires will manifest in your life. You are creating the opportunities and divine support by just knowing and believing that these things are present in your life.

Since we started with our Go to Vision, you began this exercise on a higher vibration. By doing this, you mixed up the good feelings! These visualizations are both hi-vibe feelings that raise your vibrations through the roof! We have more than one hi-vibe emotion going right now. Remember the amazing things you desire happen when your flow is high and open.

But what does all this have to do with your self perception? What if…? At some point in our lives we all have something that we desire and say: "What if?" To be honest, it probably happens frequently!

"What if" can be a good thing when we use it the right way. "What if" can also be negative if you allow it to take you into worries and fear. It won't be negative for you any longer with these tips. We'll stay on the positive side of "what if" so you can use it for your benefit.

During this period of your life, it is perfect timing to learn these practices. The positive changes, the acceptance letters, or the friendships you want to experience in your life will usher themselves in. Even though you aren't sure exactly what you want, that's okay. The point is to experience life so you know how you like to feel and how you do not like to feel.

It's much like knowing what sorts of foods you love and which you don't prefer. Had you not experienced the meal, you wouldn't have known what you wanted. Think of these manifesting practices like you are ordering off of a menu and telling the universe how you desire your life to be prepared. You would not be given dreams if you were not capable of achieving them.

So, what if?

What if I traveled to Nepal?
What if I got accepted into that college?
What if I could play that instrument well?
What if I live on the water and I could go to the ocean everyday?

It's so amazing! We are thinking outside of the box now!

it onto a high vibrational frequency so you can receive the same! Get that flow valve open!

Today's Inspired Action

Get your journal.

"What if" there was no 'what if'? Start thinking this way.

Let's begin with one possible statement and learn how to think differently about it.

Statement: "What if I got into that school where I was able to travel my entire freshman year of college?

Consider writing something like: "I am travelling through Europe and studying things that I am very passionate about. I am meeting new people and visiting art museums every weekend." (Now visualize yourself in all of these places and experiencing what you just wrote as if you are already there)

We attach a positive outcome to it. You visualize the "what if…" without the "what if…?".

You retrain your subconscious mind. Then you throw it onto a high vibrational frequency so you can receive the same! Get that flow valve open!

"What if I fall? Oh, but my darling what if you fly?"
-Erin Hanson

NOTES
for your eyes only

_____
_____
_____
_____
_____
_____
_____

Day 22
You Are Amazing

"I'm in gymnastics. I have even competed and placed at state. When I am on the bars or nailing a floor routine, I feel the absolute best about myself. It's an activity that challenges me in all the right ways and boosts my confidence. Everytime I nail a backflip, I feel amazing."
Charlotte, age 17

Yesterday, you played the "what if...?" game. We mixed up your feelings and really got your spark really going!

I hope you had a lot of fun with that. I'd like you to do it as often as you can. You can do this even sitting in a car, driving, or lying in bed. Do it whenever you can! Use all of these times for your benefit.

Get into that feeling place! Get into that 'what if?' place! Raise your vibrations and you will raise your entire life in that direction. You have the power and ability to create amazing things for yourself.

I have another question for you. What do you think you do that's amazing? This does not necessarily have to be the job that you do or a subject you excel at.

It could be that you are amazing at organization, have a great sense of humor, can cook well, or run long distances easily. It can be anything that you feel gratification and pride in. If you are a sister or daughter, it does not have to be that you think you are the best sister or good at making your parents happy. I am sure you do, but let's make this about you.

Find something that is uniquely you! Whatever comes to your mind first. Then, write it down!

I wrote down that I am good at organizing. I just am. I perceive myself as being very good at organizing and I enjoy it! I like to organize things, schedules, lives, anything!

Today's Inspired Action

Get your journal.

Write down what you are amazing at.
Meditate with that feeling and marinate in it. You should feel this way all of the time about yourself. You will find that when you do, you are more confident and more likely to jump at opportunities and more opportunities will come your way.

Remember: Play the "what if" game as often as you can! Always remember that you can go back to day 14 and re-read your letter to the universe and get excited again!

You should be excited! There are some amazing things coming your way and you are worthy and deserving of all of them.

> "Nothing can dim the light that shines from within."
> -Maya Angelou

NOTES
for your eyes only

_____
_____
_____
_____
_____
_____
_____

DAY 23
Your Worth

"My dream is to join the Peace Corps one day. I absolutely love the idea of helping impoverished countries and helping people in general. I hope to one day start a nonprofit. Sometimes, I feel like I'm not worthy of something like that. I mean, am I a good enough person?"
Jeanette, age 16

Today is a very important day. You are already seeing amazing shifts in your life right now. Even if they are small to you, celebrate each and every one! Gratitude raises your vibrations and shows the universe that you are grateful for where you are and what you have right now. The universe then knows you are open to more and will meet you halfway.

Part of receiving is believing we are worthy of that which we desire. Remember this, you will not receive that which you don't believe you are worthy of. So, getting self worth nailed down is very important in the process of creating our lives on purpose.

Today's question is, therefore, a big one: Do you think you are worthy?

Do you feel that you are worthy of the amazing public speaking. This would be an example of a type of experiences and opportunities that come your way whe you allow the flow of them? Do you feel worthy of the acceptance letter from the college you desire to go to? Do you feel worthy to enjoy and receive nice things? Do you feel worthy that the perfectly aligned relationship is in your life or on the way?

You have to know and feel that you are worthy before you see the doors open for the new opportunities waiting for you. I see it so often. People hold themselves back because they have limiting beliefs that they were given from the past or a block they gave themselves.

You might have had a bad experience in the past that makes you fearful of doing anything similar to it in the present. Perhaps you were giving a speech and you blanked halfway through. Now, you don't speak up as often as you think you should and avoid public speaking. This would be an example of a type of block.

Some of us may feel like we are not good enough, not smart enough, not this, or not that....not worthy. Whatever it is for you, remember these are just stories that your subconscious mind tells you.

I see people that are trying to do all the right things. They journal, meditate, they're good to others. They have gratitude and they still feel like they're blocked from the flow of manifesting the life that they desire. They still feel like their desires are out of reach and that they are not worthy of what they truly desire in their life.

So, do you believe you are worthy? This is a question that I would like for you to really think about. I am sure you know your answer. Be honest and clear with yourself. This is a step to the realization that you do have limiting beliefs and blocks about what you feel you "deserve."

I find that sometimes people make up excuses. For example, there may be a job you really desire and you say things like, "I am not smart enough for that" or "I do not have enough experience." You put yourself down in many ways and it becomes the predominant voice in your head. It becomes a mental habit.

Or it could be that you are afraid of success. I see a lot of this too. For me, this was a limiting belief that I had for myself and it blocked me from success. I put myself down over the years thinking that I was not smart or pretty enough.

Fear is a very real deterrent to manifesting the life you desire. It can attract circumstances and create outcomes that we don't want in our lives. Sometimes it paralyzes our ability entirely. It's important to face fear and reverse it.

I will tell you that once you get rid of that burden that you place on yourself, it is such a huge relief and you will begin to see the flow open.

I always knew that there was so much more out there for me. Once I got rid of my blocks about my worthiness, my world began to open up.

This simple thing affects so many parts of your life.

If you have a business and you fear your prices are too high, recognize where that thought actually comes from. Is it that your prices are actually too high or do you feel that you are not worthy of that amount?

Whatever your answer, what you feel about it will be exactly how others perceive it. They'll see that you or your product are not worth that amount. This is an indication that you feel you are not worthy and that it impacts your business and your life.

Ultimately, we get what we believe we are worthy of. So, when you know we have a high worth those situations and people that do not align with that worth will naturally leave your life. You will find yourself surrounded by the highest quality just by keeping the standard for yourself high.

Acknowledge it and know that it is there so that you can change it.

"Sometimes the hardest part of the journey is believing that you are worthy of the trip."
-Glen Beck

Today's Inspire Action

Get your journal.

Are you worthy?

If your answer is yes, and you truly feel that you are worthy, then that is amazing.

If you feel worthy, consider writing something like: I am worthy and deserve to experience all of the amazing opportunities and people that enter my life.

If you feel you are not worthy, consider writing the same thing: I am worthy and deserve to experience all of the amazing opportunities and people that enter my life. I am open to the flow of receiving greatness..

Make this statement a daily mantra.

● ● ● ● ● ● ● ● ● ● ● ●

NOTES
for your eyes only

_____

_____

_____

_____

_____

_____

_____

_____

_____

_____

_____

DAY 24

How You Perceive Others

"In highschool, I think everyone is concerned about what others think of them to some degree. That's because we are all looking and comparing each other. I think that if I feel like I come up short, I'll notice where others are better than me more often than not."
Christine, age 15

Today, let's think about how we perceive others. How we perceive others is actually a reflection of how we may perceive ourselves. Usually, the things we are quick to over criticize in others are the very things that we criticize ourselves for. So, paying attention to those judgments is a good road map when we are addressing our own self perception.

We may have allowed society and those around us to affect the way we live our lives. It is easy to live more from the ego self because through the years most of our subconscious minds were trained to go to the "glass half empty" mentality. We must re-train our minds to stay away from negativity and think more in a "glass half full" mentality.

It is sometimes hard to feel positive when there can be so much negativity at school and among our peers.

Please remember, that there may be things going on in someone's home life that are difficult. Perhaps they are facing a challenge you aren't aware of. If you feel that it is best to stay away from that negativity it's ok. If you feel you should lend a hand that's ok too. But know that there are resources available if a situation seems to big to handle on your own. You will find resources at the back of this book. Be sure not to feed into the cycle yourself.

What is the first thing you think of when you see somebody?

Do you automatically go towards the negative or positive? If you tend to go toward the negative about others then it is time to become aware of this and figure out why. Be more conscious of how you perceive other people and how open you are to others'

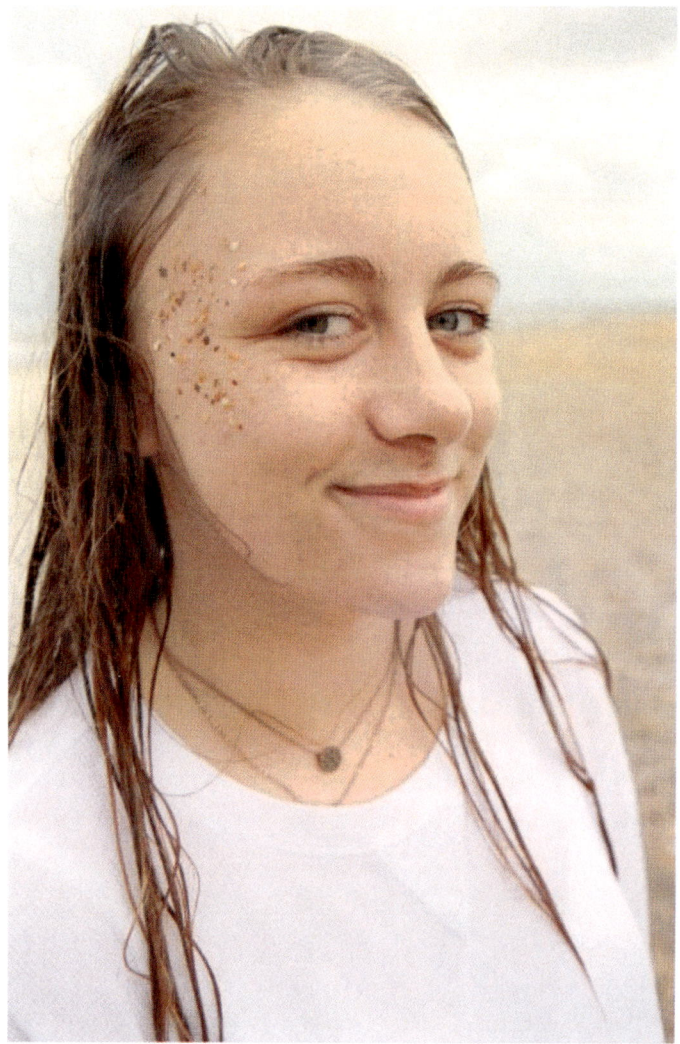

opinions.

Do you automatically judge people? Bring awareness to your thought process. If it is judgmental, it negatively affects you everyday and colors what you bring into your life. This type of energy is very low frequency.

Remember, what you put out, you will get back on the same frequency.

I am not saying to be naive and that everyone and everyday is sunshine and roses. But what is your typical first thought? Is it: "Her shirt is so unique", or is it "I can't believe she left the house looking like that"?

It is important to remember that not everyone is on the same path as you. Be open to everyone's unique path. Also remember that if you are a harsh critic of others, you may be a harsh critic of yourself too. Think about what kind of energy you are radiating out in that case. This should prompt you to change.

Today's Inspired Action

Get your journal.

How do you perceive others? Do you lean towards judgment or do you look for the best in people first?

If you lean towards judgmental, consider writing something like: I will look at people with positive thoughts first from now on. I honor and appreciate their path just as I honor and appreciate mine.

Now, take it one step further. Whenever you first meet someone, always think about something positive that is unique to them at that time. Something like: "I love her blouse, it's a beautiful color" or "His eyes look so caring".

Have a fall back, maybe you always look at someone's smile first. There is always something.

> "Remember, everyone has a story behind them. Everyone is going through different things in their life. Remember this before you choose to judge anyone."
> -Cathlene Miner

NOTES
for your eyes only

Day 25
Complimenting Yourself

"It's so easy for me to compliment others, but it's really hard for me to grasp the concept of complimenting myself. I suppose I might count on other people to do that. When they don't, it does make me feel badly. I think that if I got into the habit of doing that I wouldn't rely on the opinions of others so much."
Beverly, age 14

The person that should compliment you the most is… you. The only one that matters is you. If you have a high opinion of yourself, nobody can shake you. No, you are not being selfish! We are the base of what is happening in our lives, right?!

I know so many times you will ask other people something like, "What do you think of my…?" We all know we've done it! But it really shouldn't matter. Why do we really desire to know anyone else's opinion about our appearance?

Whatever your answer is to this, it is going to tell you a whole lot about how you radiate out your energies.

Are you looking for acceptance?
Are you looking for attention?
Are you trying to soothe an insecurity?
Are you looking for validation?

We should never let another person's opinion dictate how we feel about ourselves. I see this so often!

If you do ask those questions, do you allow that person's response to dictate how you perceive yourself? Do you allow it to dictate how your day or night will go?

Remember, how we perceive ourselves dictates our energy frequency. Waiting for someone else to tell us how we should feel is just crazy. It also means that we are always going to be up and down and all over the place as others are dictating our emotions. This is not the way that the universe desires us to work. When you do this you aren't meeting the universe halfway. You stall your progress. Would you tell your sibling or a loved one to base their day or life on what "everyone" else thinks?

I am sure the answer is, NO.

Another thing to realize is that when we have a poor image of ourselves, we sometimes paint the actions or opinions of others in a way that they did not mean. We almost search for negativity in comments because that is what we are telling ourselves. So, when we are complimenting ourselves we will find positive comments and actions coming to us more often.

We must not wait for others to make us feel good. We give ourselves compliments because we give ourselves what we desire. We bring in our desired outcomes. By living this way, you aren't allowing anyone else to dictate how you are radiating out your energy.

Compliment yourself more than anybody else does! If I knew the things that I know now back then, what a difference it would have made. I learned many lessons and I would not change a single thing, but wow!

Now I am able to help others too and it's all good.

I know that I am in control of how I feel. How I feel about myself gives me a whole different perspective! I look at this universe and situations in a totally different way than I did in the past and it shows. I compliment myself multiple times everyday.

What a weight off of my shoulders, and it will be for you too!

Today's Inspired Action

Get your journal.

Think of something about your appearance or personality that you always ask for someone's opinion on. Write down what you desire to hear them say.

Now you can answer your own question.

Remember that it's you that should be complimenting you the most. Fly high on those vibrations! Allow the excitement to bubble up inside!

> "Love yourself enough to loosen your grip and let go of what needs to be freed."
> -Alex Elle

NOTES
for your eyes only

> Dreams do come true, we just have to work hard enough. Stay focused amongst the chaos of life. Enjoy yourself, after all we only live once.
> - Enna

Day 26
Dreaming and Manifesting

"I dream every single night and I love it. I even have a journal by my bed that I write my dreams in every morning so I don't forget them. Sometimes things even happen in my waking life that I have already dreamt! If I could create the life I wanted through my dreams, that would be amazing. I mean, I'm already half way there, right?"
Bethany, age 17

When we sleep our subconscious mind works overtime. It's usually about either the things that we heard before we went to bed or that we saw throughout the day.

What you think about before you go to bed is really important. What do you focus on before you drift off to sleep? What is the last think you typically think about before you go to bed?

Relaxing and getting on that high energy frequency vibration before you go to sleep is key. You can manifest and create the life you desire in your sleep (literally) with this practice.
I know relax and high vibe sound like it may be contradicting. But, if it is the high vibe feeling that feels right it is relaxing.

Do you desire to feel different in the morning? Use this practice as yet another way you can create and manifest the things that you desire in your life. Feel yourself "being there" that place and or situation that you desire as you drift off. See situations falling into place. Whether it's about school, your friendships, your home, a situation within a relationship...anything!

For over 26 years I've told my personal training client to visualize how they desire to be. How do you desire to look and feel? Visualize this before you go to bed at night. Really feel it.

Maybe you desire to live in the mountains or, more specifically, on a mountaintop. Imagine sitting on a bench, hearing the birds, and seeing the clouds up close and personal. Maybe you desire to live at the beach. Listen and hear the waves as you drift off to sleep. Feel yourself at the beach and visualize it.

You are there.

Either make it about you or something that will truly get you excited. See how it changes what you think when you wake up in the morning and how your days flow!

If you are not purposefully manifesting anything specific in your life right now (why not?!) then think of what you are grateful for - truly heartfelt and soulfully grateful. Have whatever you are grateful for be about you since you are doing the 30 Day Self Perception Makeover right now.
Visualize that as you drift off to sleep.

You surely have something you are grateful for. Look back at day 20 or 21. What are you truly grateful for about you?

Think about this for at least 18 seconds.

Today's Inspired Action

Get your journal.

What thoughts do you think before you close your eyes at night?

Write down what you will visualize for the next week every night as you drift off to sleep. Remember, it takes at least 18 seconds for this to stick into your subconscious mind.

Then, start every day with an attitude of gratitude.

Be sure to also surround yourself with comforting objects and sounds. Try to stay off of your cell phone and electronic devices as much as possible a few hours before bedtime. This helps you to get to sleep faster with a clearer open mind and also sleep much more soundly.

"Gratitude is the healthiest of all human emotions. The more you express gratitude for what you have, the more likely you will have even more to express gratitude for."
-Zig Ziglar

Notes
for your eyes only

DAY 27
What Others Think

"My parents are my greatest supporters and cheerleaders. Whenever I'm feeling down and out they always have a way of bringing me back up again. My mom usually tells me how talented I am and my dad reminds me of my beauty."
Courtney, age 14

Have you ever wondered about what the ones closest to you love about you? Other people can see the amazing things in you that you cannot. I'm not talking about what casual friends or acquaintances think. We have people in our lives that are there through thick and thin. Those who see us from the inside out. These are the individuals I'm speaking of.

Now, asking those closest to us how they perceive us in our entirety isn't the same as asking for their opinion about something trivial like our personal style! We want to know what attracted them to us, or what quality they love about us.

So, let's ask!

Today's Inspired Action

Get your journal.

Ask your best friend, sibling, grandparent, or parent (anyone that really knows you) what they love or value about you. While you are at it, make sure you tell them what you love about them!

Finish this sentence:
People love me because I am (fill in the blank).

Recognize how valuable you are to the lives of so many. Even when you feel as if you aren't doing very much sometimes, understand that just by existing you are adding so much to the lives of those around you. Sometimes we feel as if we have to be making big strides or grand gestures in order to be valuable to others.

This isn't true. The most important thing you can ever do in this life is to just be you. Somedays, that means you're doing a lot. Other days, it's just being there. Either way, look at how much love and value you bring to those closest to you and the world.

> Taking time out everyday to feel grateful for my family and friends makes me smile. And I know smiling is good...Really Good...Malina

NOTES
for your eyes only

_____
_____
_____
_____
_____
_____
_____
_____
_____
_____
_____
_____

Day 28
Your Empty Space

"I have taken away a lot from this book already, but I feel a little off I suppose. I feel like I've let so much go through this process, but there nothing there to fill the space back up. It's hard not going back to old habits and old ways of thinking."
Genny, age 17

As you've seen during the last 27 days, great self perception includes connecting within. This may trigger a sort of spiritual awakening as you raise your energy vibrational frequency. This awakening just means that you are becoming more in tune with a source that has always been there, you are just now realizing more and more of its presence in your life. At the same time, you are learning to use it!

However, these feelings are not always a ray of sunshine. They can involve some painful realizations of limiting beliefs, blocks, and trapped negative emotions. You may be left with empty spaces that "feel" they must be filled. This can be emotionally exhausting, but it's actually making more room for that which will serve you as opposed to that which has kept you in some negative cycles.

It's a good thing!

Know that you are making space for the amazing things you've been waiting for to come into your life. Those gaps you feel will be filled soon. So, be grateful for the spaces. It's like you are renovating your house and adding a beautiful addition!

The lessons that we learn in this life are so valuable. Nothing is ever truly a failure or a negative unless we allow it to be labeled that. The more we become aware, learn the lessons we need to through our experiences, and let go of negative energies, the more room it leaves for an amazing high energy vibration to fill the space. AND, that high energy vibration may be the very situation, opportunity or thing you have been desiring. When we resist these changes and do not choose to move forward it can cause depression, anxiety, pain, and so on.

By letting go, learning our lessons, and moving on,

we connect with the universe by vibrating at a high energy. This allows us to live our best life. It also allows to us to heal ourselves and permanently change that which kept us in cycles that weren't allowing for us to move forward. Once you feel your soul connect, partial love for yourself will no longer be enough. You will know that in this life it all starts with self perception and believing in yourself.

Love you for you and where you are right now in this space, is the place to begin. Right now, you are exactly where you need to be. There is more out there. You know that you can love you. You know this life is limitless.

Everyone who has made it to this point has had a situation that has challenged them to think about the path they are on in their lives. We sometimes forget about what is truly on the inside when we focus so much on the outside.

Today's Inspired Action

Get your journal.

What lesson turned you around and reminded you that it was time to connect to your intuition? Perhaps focus on a situation you once perceived as negative, but now you understand how much it taught you.

What are you grateful for about it? Write this down.

Side note: Sometimes it's hard to be grateful for things that have happened in our lives that left us feeling pain, heartache, or even betrayal. Think of pain as a navigator. It is there to show us the areas of our lives where something needs healing or something needs to change.

> "Yesterday, I was clever, so I wanted to change the world. Today, I am wise, I am changing myself."
> -Rumi

Notes
for your eyes only

Day 29
Life and Lessons

"I'm so excited for the future. Even though sometimes it might be a bit scary, I know that whatever I set my mind to I will be able to dominate. All I really want to do is make a positive impact on the world doing the thing that I really love."
Whitney, age 15

Learning how your brain really works on a subconscious level allows you to truly, and purposefully, manifest (create/magnetize) your desired life and opportunities. More importantly, it allows you to recognize those opportunities to take inspired action on those amazing possibilities when they present themselves.

Maybe there is something that you thought was negative, but you now see it in a positive light?

This is much like our topic yesterday. The reason I am bringing this up is because how we face and feel through challenges will affect how we react and make choices through them. Feeling negative about challenge usually yields negative results. It is important to understand that we grow through challenge.

Facing challenges with an open mind and willingness to learn and grow through them means that we are in control. When we allow emotion to take over and begin to feel like nothing is going to work in our favor, we have handed over the keys. We are no longer driving.

Today's Inspired Action

Get your journal.

This is your focus for today: What is that one BIG take away that stands out in your mind from the last 28 days?

Write that down and then celebrate!

"Knowing yourself is the beginning of all wisdom."
-Aristotle

NOTES
for your eyes only

Day 30
Forgiving Yourself

"There are things that I do regret. I've chosen to opt out of extracurricular activities just because I didn't have the time even though I knew it would probably benefit me. I've also regretted how I have reacted to some situations with my friends."
Laramie, age 17

Whatever is on your mind on a day to day basis is directly correlated to the energy vibrations that you send out. It is so important to be aware of the "why" behind our thoughts.

What is that "thing" that you need to forgive yourself for?

Self-forgiveness is a block that we many not recognize at first, but it is one of the most important and common. Instead of forgiving ourselves for different actions or thoughts, most tend to push it to the back of the minds and ignore it. This keeps us from forgiving ourselves and healing within. Do you ever notice that most of us are more quick to forgive others than we are to forgive ourselves.

Just because we wish something never happened doesn't mean it didn't. We must acknowledge that we may have needed certain events to occur to teach us certain lessons in life. We can learn a lot from the things that didn't go our way, if we just let ourselves.

Forgiveness allows us to nurture that place within us and allows it to heal, grow, and evolve. Think of that something that you need to forgive yourself for (or heal from) and accept that it happened. Give yourself credit for getting through it. Recognize that it taught you a lesson and gave you the ability to delve deeper into yourself.

Now it is time to forgive yourself and heal so you can move on. By doing this, you unblock your flow, open up your world, and see shifts happen right before your eyes.

You cannot change that it happened. So, forgive yourself and take that weight off of your shoulders. It is really okay. It is over.

Today's Inspired Action

Get your journal.

Today, write what you forgave yourself for. Be sure to write specifically about what you have forgiven and that you have released what you no longer need (make these words resonate with you).

You can now release it and begin to heal. The healing space requires zero judgment and criticism. Imagine it is a place of healing light.

Bonus: On the next full moon and new moon, use the moon's energies to help manifest and rid yourself of blocks, limiting beliefs, and forgive yourself for past events. For more information on the full moon and new moon rituals, visit my website.

www.cathleneminer.com/30day

NOTES
for your eyes only

_____
_____
_____
_____
_____
_____
_____
_____
_____
_____
_____

Bonus Day

Your Self Confidence

"I feel very confident in myself most days. There are sometimes when I don't, but I think everyone has bad days. The point is to never stay in your bad day. Always stay positive!"
Shelbie, age 17

Now, let's think about self confidence and what it is. Webster's Dictionary defines it as: "confidence in oneself and in one's powers and abilities."

So many people credit the amount of confidence they have in themselves to their outward definition of success. What grades am I making? How many friends to I have? How many likes do I have on Instagram? How many followers do I have?
Self confidence is built on so many different things working together, but overall, it is build on your self perception.

Think about it. It has everything to do with how you think and feel about you. Your self perception dictates your personal version of success. It dictates how high you aim and how far you will take it. It dictates what you will "settle" for (I do not encourage settling at all). And, of course, it dictates the choices you make.

Think ahead a year or so, How many likes you had on a post will not matter at all!!

First, you must know what your version of success looks like and how you use your passions to get you there. The passion you have for something often translates to how much fuel you have to get the job done. Remember as well, that your version of success is achieved through a process. The finish line is won by the race. As a teenager, your race is just beginning.

However, you'll experience many wins on the way. Your version of success will change throughout the years too!

Taking the time to discover these things is one of the most worthwhile uses of your time in life. I know that you have been inspired during these past 30 days and now know what really lights you up and what feeling you do not desire to feel.

Self confidence is believing in yourself enough to make decisions without needing external guidance to confirm your choices (a trusted adult figure for advice is always welcome).Know when you aren't being treated with respect (we receive what we think we deserve). Stand up for yourself by doing what is right no matter what the crowd is doing.

When you started this journey 30 days ago, you self confidence may not have been soaring. Where are you now? What is one thing that you can say you are "super" confident about now?

When you have confidence, true confidence, you know that the only thing that matters is what you think about yourself. You are 100% confident in your decisions because you can feel that you are aligned with your intuition. So, you trust your intuition your "gut" 100 %.

As you make the important decisions that are shaping your future, have confidence in what you have learned thus far in this book and build upon it. Your life will not always go along the way you planned, but remember that this is okay. When you hear a "no", it is not a "never". It simply means "not this way" or "not right now". There may be something right around the corner that you will love even more! You are still attracting what you need to create the life that you desire.

You also no longer compare yourself to others. You may look up to someone or admire them, but comparing is a thing of the past.

When you have a healthy self perception, everything falls into place as you desire because you learn to trust your intuition 100% of the time. Your intuition leads you on the path to your passions. Sometimes that means taking risks not many would and living a life that is "outside of the box".

As you go through life, remember, that you will make important decisions and set boundaries for yourself. There may be some people that feel threatened by your confidence. You do not have to take ownership of how your decisions make them feel.

You are uniquely and beautifully you. There is no apology necessary.

Now….take on the world.

Today's Inspired Action

Get your journal.

What is one thing that you feel super self confident about now? Without a doubt you know you can do this "thing" or this "thing" is going to happen. Have no doubts when you put it on paper.

By acknowledging this and getting it from your brain and onto paper (then visualizing yourself there), you begin a chain reaction of energetic events. Be confident of your position in that chain of events and feel what it's like to be there. As you do this, you raise your energy frequency and align with the perfect path for you right now.

Photo By: Katarina Stanic

Notes
for your eyes only

Where To Go From Here...

Well!! You did it!!

Thank you for going on this journey with me. It's an amazing feeling to share the best parts of some of the work that has made a huge impact in my life, my friends' lives, my children's lives and my clients' lives throughout the years. I loved the process of writing it all down so that I can share it with you and the world. You will be connected to your intuition and ahead of most of your peers.

You did this work the last 30 days to begin your journey towards manifesting the life that you desire. You can now see how everything in this life is based on how you feel about yourself and it radiates out from there.

You can achieve anything once you know that you are limitless. Set your mind to it, visualize it, and feel it. Once you do, whatever you desire is on its way.

Whether you made big or small shifts in your life these past 30 days, I am here to celebrate each one of those with you. Now live life constantly celebrating yourself. Celebrate that paper that you finished. That project that you turned in. The help that you gave your parents and or teachers.

If you followed each day, showed up for yourself, followed through, and took Inspired Action, look back and observe how far you have come. Now that you have a better self perception, your entire world shifts in your favor. It is important to keep it up!

These 30 days were an absolutely amazing start but the journey is not over yet. It is important to keep journaling and meditating. Think of that GO TO Vision that you journaled about. Recall it right now or anytime you feel energetically low.

It is important to keep practicing that feeling so you have it at the ready and can use it. Use your bag of tricks when you feel the "funk" creeping in and you need to get yourself out of a low energy vibration.

Take a minute some days to go back to day 14 and reread your letter to the universe. Visualize and feel it as you read. Play the "what if" game as often as you can (we all love a game!).

It's exciting when you get into the place of truly feeling things positively change.
These are practices that will guide you for the rest of your life to make positive shifts and changes. Spread the word and tell a friend. Allow them to begin their journey.

I created a journaling course and book that explains the steps of journaling for the life you desire (subscribe at cathleneminer.com to get the course launch date sent). Doing the journaling course after you have put this book into practice allows even more amazing shifts in your life (I know! - it's possible!). I recommend doing the course and book. Then create your very own unique journaling practice for yourself.

It is extremely important that you revisit The 30 Day Self Perception Makeover every six months. Revisit it when you feel disconnected from the true authentic you or when the outside world begins to dictate your life.

As I mentioned in this book, you are exposed to the energy of others every day. With the ebb and flow of life, your path changes. Change is a great thing and something I definitely encourage. Just be cognizant of how those changes make you feel. If it feels right it will lead to your personal, spiritual, and financial growth throughout the years.

When you reconnect every 6 months or more you'll have a much clearer view of the path that you were put in this life to take; the path that fills your soul and keeps you reaching for more.

Remember to follow your intuition. The universe has a plan for you that is better than you could ever imagine. You can live it as long as you listen. Be quite and listen. Be sure to subscribe to my Manifesting Magic in your everyday life blog for weekly instruction and daily inspiration.

Happy Manifesting on Purpose to a Soulfully Fulfilling Life!

Cathlene Miner

Notes
for your eyes only

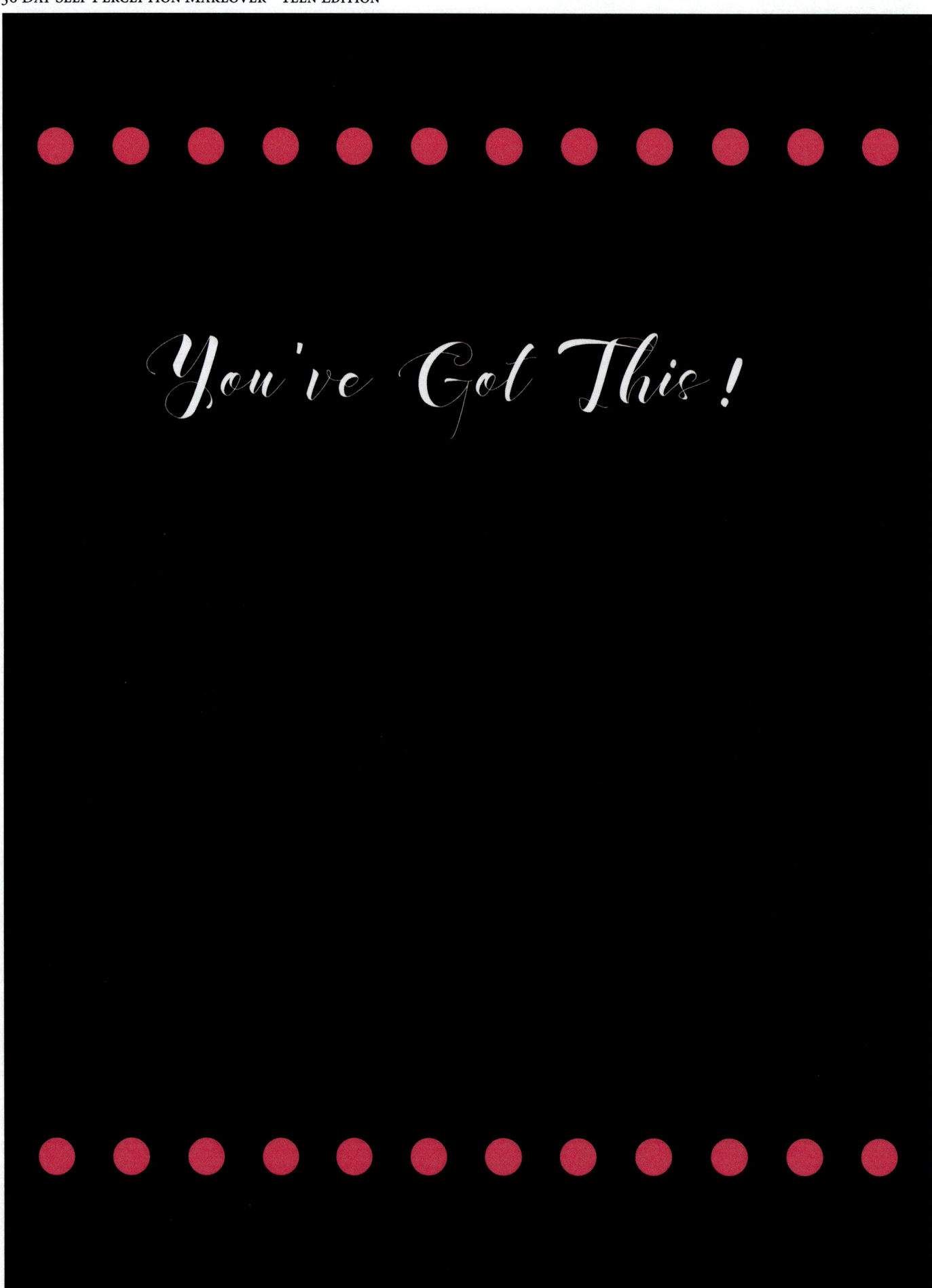

Affirmations

Positive Affirmations.

Use these affirmations as Inspiration to you. Change them up and make them your own. Pick your favorite and repeat them daily. Write them on sticky notes and place them everywhere! Use them different times throughout the day. Maybe have some on your bathroom mirror. In your lunch bag. On your computer, etc...

I am
I am important.
I am brave.
I am safe and secure.
I am beautiful.
I am strong.
I am confident.
I am worthy.
I am allowed to feel all of my feelings.
I am kind.
I am creative.
I am imaginative.

I believe I am
I believe in myself.
I am awesome!
I am allowed to feel proud of myself.
I trust myself.
I trust my intuition 100%
I listen to my heart.

Acceptance and Loving Myself
I love myself.
I accept myself.
I am worthy of my heartfelt desires.
I deserve to be happy.
I consider my own feelings.
I consider other people's feelings.
I am my own perfect.
I am worthy of every amazing opportunity that comes my way.

I can be accepted just as I am.
I love and accept all parts of myself.
I forgive myself for my mistakes and have learned by them.
I think positive thoughts about myself.
I speak to myself with kindness.
My body is strong and healthy.
I respect my body.

It's ok to be:
It's okay to be sad.
It's okay to be angry.
It's okay to be scared.
It's ok to say no.

I am grateful
I am grateful for what I have.
I am compassionate.
I am generous.
I love my body.
I am grateful for my health.
My body is perfect the way it is.
I don't compare myself to others.
I am grateful to my body.

Relationships
I help others.
I include others.
I am a good friend.
I am trustworthy.
I can be myself in my friendships.
It's ok to be different than my friends.
I am unique.
I am allowed to have all kinds of friends.
I deserve to be accepted for my true self.
I deserve to be treated with kindness.
I can be my own unique self and belong.
I am an important part of my family.
I can disagree with my family and still be loved.
I am loved.
I love my family.

I will get my life's desires

I set my own unique goals(desires).
I enjoy the journey to my goals.
I enjoy being challenged and learning.
I can make mistakes and still reach my goals.
I believe in myself.
I am consistent.
I always take inspired action.
It's ok to accept help from others on the journey to my desires, goals.
I believe in my dreams.
I can reach my dreams.
I go with the flow.
I have amazing ideas.
I am always open to new ideas.
Anything in this Universe is possible.
This Universe is limitless and my wildest dreams can come true.

I can communicate with others

I speak with kindness
I speak with respect.
I speak with strength.
I speak with courage.
I stand up for myself.
I stand up for others.
I listen with love.
I speak through love.
I have the courage to share my true feeling.
Others do not have to agree with me and that's ok.
I respect others even I do not agree with them.
I am responsible for my words.

Challenges

I can overcome any challenges.
I have a solution based approach to challenges.
I ask for help when needed.
I have support in facing my challenges.
I learn from my challenges.
Challenges make me stronger and allow me to help others.
I can handle any challenges that come my way.

Getting Peaceful and Calm

I am peaceful.
I am relaxed.
I am calm.
I let go of my worries and stressors.
I can calm my mind by going inward and feeling my breath.
I am relaxing my whole body and mind.
I feel my stressors dissolve away.

Working Together

We are all more similar than different.
Each person has something unique to contribute.
Each of us can work together to solve problems.
Together we will create peace.
Together we are the world!

> "You are only at the beginning…
> Just Imagine what else is out there waiting for you."
> - Cathlene Miner

Resources

USA

Dating Abuse
Domestic Violence
National Abuse Hotline:
The Hotline.org
1-800-799-7233

Eating Disorders
National Eating Disorders.org
1-800-931-2237

Suicide Life Line
LinesforLife.org
Suicide Life Line
1-800-273-8255 (24/7/365)
Text 273TALK to 839863 (8am-11pm PST)

Alcohol and Drug Helpline
1-800-923-4357 (24/7/365)
Text RecoveryNow to 839863 (8am-11pm PST daily)

YOUTHLINE
Call 877-968-8491
Text teen2teen to 839863
Chat at www.oregonyouthline.org

Australia

Domestic Violence
Dating Abuse
1800 RESPECT or 1800 737 732
https://au.reachout.com/articles/domestic-violence-support

Eating Disorders
https://thebutterflyfoundation.org.au/our-services/helpline/Call 1800 ED HOPE (1800 33 4673)

Suicide Life Line
https://www.lifeline.org.au/
https://www.lifeline.org.au/get-help/topics/lifeline-services

KidsHelpLine
Kidshelpline.com.au
1800 55 1800

United Kingdom

Domestic Violence/Dating Abuse
0808 2000 247

Eating Disorders
https://www.beateatingdisorders.org.uk/support-services/helplines
0808 801 0711

Suicide Life Line
Helpline: 01708 765200
https://www.supportline.org.uk/problems/suicide/

Alcohol and Drug Helpline
https://www.supportline.org.uk/problems/drugs/

Canada

Domestic Violence/Dating Abuse
1-800-579-2888

Eating Disorders
http://nedic.ca/

http://www.kidshelpphone.ca
1-800-668-6868

Suicide Life Line
http://www.crisisservicescanada.ca/
18334564566
Chat via text: 45645

If you are in need of a different resourse message us at
info@Hopefullhandbags.org
so we can connect you with the support line near you.

www.hopefullhandbags.org

"Never Underestimate the Power of Hope"-Cathlene

I started Hopefull Handbags with a mission is to give Hope to women getting back on their feet again due to Domestic Violence and other detrimental situations. We do this one handbag at a time by receiving once loved donated handbags, filling them with necessities, inspirational notes and things to make women feel amazing and donating them to women getting back on their feet again. Some of these women are staying in shelters and most with children. The smiles and the feeling of hope are priceless.

"Never Underestimate the Power of Hope".

The Handbags Full of Hope is only part of it. For Hopefull Handbags, it is also about raising awareness that Domestic Violence is real. It happens in all socioeconomic backgrounds as with other detrimental situations some women may find themselves in.

Another part of our mission is raising awareness around the world that there is Help, Hope and Support all over at no charge. The more people we can spread the word to we potentially reach the very women that need to be connected to safety. Maybe they just start with a mention to a friend and that friend directing them to us or an organization that can guide them and their children to safety.
Men are also survivors of Domestic Violence and the Detrimental Situations sometimes and they are given the same services when needed.

Hopefull Handbags, Inc. 501c3 believes in collaboration over competition. That is why all events that Hopefull Handbags hosts or partner with provide a safe, inspirational, motivational, and educational uplifting experience.
A fun setting for women to engage with their community.

Hopefull Handbags focuses on providing the knowledge, tools, and community to give Hope, Help, and Support for you to feel inspired, motivated and empowered to create a positive change in your life which affects everything and everyone around you.

**Raising Hope and Vibrational Energies,
"One Handbags at a Time"**

If You, Your Group or Business would like to get involved or partner with an event message us at info@hopefullhandbags.org

Thoughts...

I believe that the 30 Day Self Perception Makeover Edition is a perfect read for a coming of age teen ready to take on the world. It is hard for anyone to start new chapters in life but being a teenager has its own challenges. This book specializes in practicing how to be the best reflection of you that you can be. Read about how to deal with negative emotional and physically draining feelings and how to change it into positive energy to put out into the world. Start manifesting the life and future you want and make your dreams a reality. You are beautiful inside and out.
- Julia 16

I was feeling very low before I began this 30 Day journey. I feel like a weight has been lifted once I began to think of my self as being enough. - Susan 16

Step out of your shell, you are made beautifully and perfectly in the eyes of the creator. When you go out in this world, don't be conformed into it, but transform it!! (Romans 12:2) You are so so loved.- Madie 17

High School can be tough. People can make you feel really bad about yourself. I realized as I went through my journey with this book that it doesn't matter how others feel about you. If it doesn't feel right they are not your people. Thank you, Cathlene and Taelor! - Carla 17

My daughter went through the 30 Day Self Perception makeover Teen Edition after I realized what a huge impact the 30 Day Self Perception Makeover had on my life. Both of us are now experiencing amazing flow in our lives and so many things are falling into place.
I highly recommend it! - Debbie, mom of Samantha 16

I feel like nowadays we get too involved with all the negativity in this world. For example, social media. Social media should be a place for influencing and spreading positivity. However, I've noticed from past experience and seeing others that we tend to use it in a negative light. For instance, we are in a constant battle with ourselves and others trying to compare to one another and competing to see who can get the most likes on a post. As a result, we begin to lose who we are and forget what truly makes us happy. Therefore, The 30 Day Self Perception Makeover is the ideal book for people who are struggling to be themselves or who need that extra light in their life! It's honestly perfect for anyone and it only takes a few minutes out of your day. Let's take on this obstacle and create a new and improved life of your own!! "Create your own sunshine" -Kaylee 17

Made in the USA
Monee, IL
12 September 2020